the vegan
Air Fryer

the vegan Air Fryer

The Healthier Way to Enjoy Deep-Fried Flavors

JL Fields

Vegan Heritage Pres

VEGAN HERITAGE PRESS, LLC
Woodstock • Virginia

ISBN: 978-1-941252-36-9
First Edition, June 2017
10 9 8 7 6 5 4

Vegan Heritage Press, LLC books are available at quantity discounts. For ordering information, please visit our website at www.veganheritagepress.com or write the publisher at Vegan Heritage Press, LLC, P.O. Box 628, Woodstock, VA 22664-0628.

Library of Congress Cataloging-in-Publication Data

Names: Fields, JL, author.
Title: The vegan air fryer : the healthier way to enjoy deep-fried flavors /
  JL Fields.
Description: Woodstock, Virginia : Vegan Heritage Press, LLC, 2017. |
  Includes index.
Identifiers: LCCN 2017004047| ISBN 9781941252369 (pbk.) | ISBN 9781941252383
  (prc)
Subjects: LCSH: Vegan cooking. | Hot air frying. | LCGFT: Cookbooks.
Classification: LCC TX837 .F4448 2017 | DDC 641.5/636--dc23 LC record available at https://lccn.loc.gov/2017004047

Photo credits: Cover and interior food photos by Michelle Donner. Back cover photos (from left): Beany Jackfruit Taquitos, page 54; Parsnip Fries, page 71; Fried Hot Dogs with Barbecue Potato Chips, page 115; and Fried Ginger-O's, page 168. Additional decorative images from stock photo sources.

Disclaimer: The information in this book is correct and complete to the best of our knowledge. The information provided in this book should not be taken as medical advice. If you require a medical diagnosis or prescription, or if you are contemplating any major dietary change, consult a qualified health-care provider. Neither the publisher nor the author are responsible for readers' health issues. The publisher is not responsible for specific health or allergy issues regarding ingredients used in this book.

Vegan Heritage Press, LLC books are distributed by Andrews McMeel Publishing.
Printed in the United States of America

Dedication

For the animals. Always.

Contents

Preface

When I was a new vegan, I discovered I didn't have to spend my life in the kitchen to eat healthy, home-cooked vegan foods. A pressure cooker could deliver plant-based basics in no time. That revelation led me to write *Vegan Pressure Cooking: Delicious Beans, Grains, and One-Pot Meals in Minutes*. I thought I had all the help I needed.

But I was wrong. I realized I needed another quick and easy cooking method to prepare great vegan food. Enter the air fryer. This fairly compact convection cooker uses rotating, rapidly moving hot air to cook food until it's crispy. However, the air fryer itself requires no oil—it's the cook's choice as to whether to add oils to food before cooking, making air-frying a much healthier alternative to traditional deep-frying.

Prior to discovering this new device, I had never fried food. Not because I don't like fried foods. I do. But I live in a cozy condo with high ceilings and horrible kitchen venting. Frying foods is smelly, messy, and downright impractical in such a setting. But when I found there was a simple, mess-free, and healthy way to make fried foods at home, I impulsively purchased an air fryer.

When the air fryer arrived, my husband, Dave, rolled his eyes. "Are you kidding me?" (He thinks I have a kitchen appliance problem.)

I huffed at Dave and marched into the kitchen. Without reading the manual (which I don't advise), I sliced a potato into pieces and pressed the fries button on the device. Twenty minutes later, I placed a plate of hot, crispy, home-cooked French fries in front of my skeptical husband. After one bite, Dave exclaimed, "This is the best thing you've ever purchased!"

Another convert was born. If you, like my husband, are doubting that air-fried goodies can taste just as good as deep-fried foods while being healthier and easier to prepare, I invite you to dive into this book. The air fryer may make a convert of you, too.

1

I'm a vegan cooking coach, and 98 percent of my clients come to me for one reason: to make vegan cooking easy. That's why for years I've taught thousands of people how to use a pressure cooker. And now I take my pressure cooker and my air fryer into my clients' homes to show them that wholesome, plant-based meals can be cooked up in no time. This cookbook is filled with mostly whole-foods recipes that are quick to make. (By the way, I consider tofu and seitan whole foods; tofu is made from soybeans and seitan has been used as a meat substitute for centuries.) But the air fryer is also great for vegan convenience foods. Pick up any meatless patty from the frozen food section of your grocery store, set the air fryer to 390°F, and in ten minutes your entrée is done!

Air Fryer 101

*A*ir fryers have been popular in Europe for years. In fact, in 2010, the *Daily Mail* in the UK wrote about this convection-cooking technology—where hot air as high as 400°F circulates around the food—because it was news. Browned, crispy foods with little to no oil cooked in minutes? What a great idea for the health-conscious consumer.

Air-Frying: The Healthier Choice

Many people are turning to a plant-based diet to lower cholesterol, reverse diabetes, and prevent heart disease. Some individuals also choose to omit oil from their cooking. The Physicians Committee for Responsible Medicine (PCRM.org) offers excellent suggestions on how to do this:

- Cook with vegetable broth or water.
- Use nonstick cooking spray.
- Use spices instead of added oils to flavor foods.
- Use applesauce in baked recipes.

Throughout this book, I defer to nonstick cooking spray as a low-oil option. I also use lots of spices and seasonings, and, yes, applesauce will be found in several of the baked goods.

This vegan cookbook is not a diet book. For those of you who are not concerned about added oils—or are actually wondering what all the fuss is about—I turned to my friend Ginny Messina, who is a nutritionist and my coauthor of *Vegan for Her: The Woman's Guide to Being Healthy and Fit on a Plant-Based Diet*. I asked her to share her thoughts on the role of oil in a healthy vegan diet, as well as her advice on the best oils. You can read what she has to say in *How to Use Oils in a Healthy Vegan Diet* (page 176).

Air-Frying Is Clean and Cool

In addition to wanting a shortcut in the kitchen, there were two other major, divergent motivators for me to invest in an air fryer. First, the cleanup is a breeze. Second, speaking of breeze, I live in an old condo with no air conditioning. When I use an air fryer, I'm able to bake, roast, grill, and fry without turning on the oven or stove and without overheating my kitchen.

Air-Frying Can Dazzle Nonvegan Friends and Family

For many new vegans, the transition to plant-based foods takes some getting used to. Many textures we're accustomed to are elusive. One way to encourage our nonvegan family and friends to eat more plants is to find foods that are familiar. Air-frying adds a crunch, a crispiness, and a meatiness that is reminiscent of our pre-vegan days. Vegan fried chicken, crispy bacon, and meaty fajitas are sure to impress.

Air Fryer Accessories

Not all air fryers are the same and not all air fryers offer the same accessories. If you become as cuckoo for air-frying as I am, you'll probably want to think about getting a grill pan or a rack to allow multiple layers of cooking. And oven-safe pans and dishes are handy for casseroles, desserts, seitan, and more. You'll see mention of specific accessories in some of the recipes. Common accessories made specifically for the air fryer include the following items:

- **Double-layer racks:** This accessory allows you to double the cooking capacity in the air fryer when cooking foods in a single layer.

- **Skewers:** The Philips brand rack has notches for stainless steel skewers. With double capacity, you can cook tofu or tempeh steaks on the bottom of the basket and place vegetable kabobs on the top layer.

- **Baskets with lids:** Philips also makes a "variety basket" with a lid for their Viva line of air fryers that is ideal for keeping food (such as kale chips) from flying up into the heating element.

- **Baking pans:** There are a variety of sizes of baking pans made for air fryers. These work well with casseroles, roasted vegetables, and cakes.

- **Baking trays:** The shallower baking trays work well for pancakes.

- **Grill pans:** The Philips brand air fryer basket is wire mesh and some foods, like tofu and battered foods, can stick. A grill insert, with a nonstick surface, is a solution.

In lieu of purchasing accessories specifically made for an air fryer, you may have small oven-safe dishes that will do the trick, such as springform pans, tortilla molds, stainless steel taco stands, ramekins, cast iron crocks, and more.

Air-Frying Can Be Healthy (or Not!)

Here's the bottom line on air-frying and your health: Everything in this book is going to fall in the "healthier than . . . " column when comparing it to a nonvegan food. But some of the recipes will never be labeled as health food (remember, this isn't a diet book). For instance, fried sandwich cookies just needed to happen here. But so did simple roasted Brussels sprouts. The recipes here are as diverse as those of you reading this book.

All About Air Fryers

As mentioned earlier, air-frying is essentially convection cooking—very hot air quickly circulating around the food. There are many air fryers on the market. I used an extra-large Philips, a smaller GoWISE, and an even smaller Farberware while creating recipes for this book. Not all air fryers are the same. Some are very powerful—to the point that flour, spices, and even pieces of kale blow into the air while cooking. Others are quiet and less formidable. Price points vary vastly, too. Some are as high as $300 while others are under $70.

Which air fryer is the right one for you? It all depends. You'll want a size that accommodates your family. If your family consists of just one or two people, a 3.2- to 3.7-quart will do just fine. If your family has four or more individuals, you're going to want a 5-quart (or larger) device.

Earlier air fryers used a paddle to move food through the convection-cooking process. Now the air is moved through the device, removing the need for the paddle, and most modern air fryers do not use one. For the purposes of this cookbook, I've written recipes for air fryers without paddles. If you have an air fryer with a paddle, review the owner's manual, because it's possible that the paddle is removable.

Another difference in air fryer models is the heating elements: halogen and coil elements. Halogen heat uses light (therefore, radiant heat), while devices with coil elements and rapid air

Air-Frying Helpers

Here is a list of helpful pieces of equipment that may already be in your kitchen to help when air-frying:

- Teflon-friendly tongs
- Air fryer–safe pans
- Air fryer–safe dishes and bowls (a variety of ramekins up to 5 or 7 inches, depending upon the size of your air fryer)
- Silicone cooking gloves
- Nonstick cooking sprays or misting canisters for spritzing
- Air fryer grill pan
- Skewers for foods such as kabobs and corn dogs

use the fan to circulate the heat. This isn't a better-or-worse comparison; rather, it's something for you to consider as you review air fryers before purchasing. In the Resources (page 175), I outline a variety of air fryers to make your decision-making process a bit easier.

When deciding on which air fryer to purchase, note that many air fryer baskets are nonstick. If that is a concern for you, consider one that uses a ceramic coating (Simply Ming brand at a lower price point) or a mesh basket (Philips brand at a higher price point).

What You Can Expect in the Recipes

You should know what I'm not: a fancy cook or trained chef. And what I am: a home cook, a cooking coach, and a faculty member of a university culinary program. These distinctions are important to understanding my approach to the recipes in this book—I simply want to help people make delicious vegan food that's easy to prepare, so that more and more people will eat vegan food. (Yep, I have an agenda.)

In this book, I'm offering no-fuss, easy-peasy, let's-get-this-food-on-the-table-already recipes. I have created recipes that are fun, delicious, and that I believe will empower you, the home cook, to make delicious vegan recipes that will please even the omnivores in your life.

What You'll Find in the Recipe Chapters

These recipes are inherently low-oil. However, I will provide notations regarding no-oil (and sometimes lower-oil) techniques and options for most recipes. I am a huge fan of spray oils for air-frying. (If you're environmentally conscious, you may want to buy an oil mister or two that relies on pumping mechanisms rather than chemical propellants.) For the purposes of this book, we are following the assumption that one (1-second) spray of oil is equivalent to about 1/4 teaspoon oil. Low-oil in this case will range from 1 to 4 sprays (rarely over 1 teaspoon for 4 servings). Alternatively, I will call for 1/4 to 1 teaspoon oil when using a marinade or when preparing some foods.

In the Resources (page 175), I provide a list of convenience foods that can easily be prepared in the air fryer, because sometimes we are too busy to even cook super-fast air fryer food!

Terms, Techniques, and Heads-Ups

Shake: This is a common term for air-frying meaning that halfway through the cooking time—or every few minutes—you'll simply need to shake the basket to move the food around and avoid sticking.

Preheat: Most air fryer manuals call for preheating. I don't always preheat, and you don't have to either. But when a recipe calls for it, give it a shot. It will help in the cooking process, but it's no big deal if you don't preheat. The cooking just might take a bit longer.

Spritz: I'm going to suggest spray oil as a low-oil option throughout the book. When I say, "spritz," I'm suggesting a quick, one-second spray of oil.

Parchment paper: For battered foods, and for oil-free alternatives to recipes, I often recommend using parchment paper. Note that you do not want big pieces of paper exposed in the air fryer. Once the parchment paper is in place, cut it down until only 1/2 inch is exposed above the base of the air fryer basket.

Size: Some recipes will do far better in a larger air fryer than a smaller one. I will make a point to mention size when I think it's an issue. And I'll offer suggestions. For instance, the Breakfast (Pan)Cake recipe (page 26) does really well in an 8-inch springform pan. Not everyone will be using an air fryer that large, so I'll make a point to mention how you can divide the recipe to accommodate a small oven-safe dish.

Serving sizes: Speaking of size, many of these recipes are for two to four people, because most air fryers aren't really designed to feed eight to ten people. You can easily double recipes but there's a good chance you'll also need to cook in batches.

Temperature: Some air fryers heat up to 400°F, others only as high as 390°F. Some can be programmed in increments of ten degrees, others in thirty. Use the closest temperature to the one I recommend in a recipe.

Notes on Safety

Air fryers get hot (that's why they are so magical). But high heat is no joke and I want you to pay heed to a few things:

- Some food may fly up into the heating element (e.g., kale chips, light tortillas) due to the force of the rapidly circulating hot air. Like any hot element in your kitchen, you'll want to tend to your device to keep an eye on these lighter foods that can actually begin smoking. This doesn't mean you have to avoid cooking these foods, it just means pay attention! There are some accessories that cover a basket to keep foods down. When making kale chips, I make a point to massage the oil into the greens to weight them down.

- Skewers are wonderful for making kabobs and keeping pieces of bread in place when making a grilled cheese sandwich. Metal is best. If you're going to use a wooden skewer or toothpick, soak it in water for twenty minutes before using it and make sure that it is several inches away from the heating element.

- Parchment paper and foil are great for cooking battered food or other food that might stick to the basket. Always cut the paper or foil to fit exactly on the bottom of the air fryer basket, with no excess paper hanging out.

- A double-layer accessory, when placed in the basket, provides a second cooking surface. Avoid cooking lightweight foods (e.g., leafy greens, tortillas) on this top rack as it's a mere inch or two away from the heating element.
- Consider investing in a pair of silicone cooking gloves. The space in the air fryer basket is tight and when using accessories you've got some maneuvering to do.

When using an air fryer, be sure to move it away from walls, positioning the vent to an open space. The intense heat can damage walls, surfaces, and other materials.

Air-Fried Foods in Your Diet

Though I'm not opposed to eating an entirely air-fried meal, keep in mind that this cookbook is offering a fun way to add texture and variety to the foods you eat. It's not a meal planner. But here are some fun ways to add air-fried foods to a well-balanced vegan diet:

Breakfast: Make tofu scramble in your skillet while air-frying Basic Breakfast Potatoes (page 22).

Lunch: Prepare the fragrant Balsamic Herbed Tomatoes (page 68) to add to a hummus wrap for lunch.

Dinner: Make the Roasted Brussels Sprouts (page 76) to add to a bowl of rice and beans for a special "hippie" bowl of beans, greens, and grains.

Dessert: Prepare Roasted Cherries Jubilee (page 163) to serve over your favorite homemade or store-bought vegan ice cream.

But, hey, if you really want to make an entire meal in the air fryer, chapter 7 is dedicated to one-basket meals!

Now that we've covered the basics of air-frying, let's cover the other emphasis of this book: veganism.

*B*elieve it or not, the word *vegan* is still confusing to some people. Certain vegetarians will say they eat fish. Others, who identify as plant-based, eat eggs from backyard chickens. No judgment here, but I want to be crystal clear about the term and what it means to me and the recipes in this book.

Vegan Basics

*E*nglishman Donald Watson is considered a founder of the modern vegan movement. In 1944, he was part of the first Vegan Society and coined the term *vegan,* meaning "a way of living that seeks to exclude, as far as possible and practicable, all forms of exploitation of, and cruelty to, animals for food, clothing and any other purpose. For the purposes of this book, *vegan* means a diet containing no animal flesh, no dairy, and no honey.

The other reason *vegan* can be confusing is because some people practice veganism—or plant-based eating—for health reasons and within that context identify their diet as "whole-foods, plant-based," avoiding the term *vegan*. For further dietary reasons, they might also exclude one or more of the following: vegetable oils, salt, sugar, soy, gluten, and even nuts and seeds. I want to point out that all of those foods are vegan and are used in this cookbook. Options abound, however, to omit or reduce some of these ingredients to accommodate such dietary choices.

To recap, vegan equals no animal products. That's it!

Ingredients to Know

Now on to a few vegan ingredients that are used in this book.

Black Salt

Also called *kala namak,* this salt is mined from the Himalayan region. And it's actually pink in color, not black. It has an aroma and flavor that is remarkably similar to hardboiled eggs. I use black salt in vegan egg dishes to enhance the flavor and to create an aroma reminiscent of eggs. Black salt can be found at Indian and Asian Pacific markets as well as online.

Chickpea (Garbanzo Bean) Flour

Naturally gluten-free, this flour is high in protein, iron, and fiber. Naturally dense, it's helpful in recipes that require some level of binding. I use it in seitan as well as in sauces and as a dry coating for some of the recipes that are battered or are destined to be a crunchy food. This flour is often sold in the bulk section of grocery stores or packaged in the baking section.

Dulse Flakes

This red sea vegetable is found in shakers in the Asian section of the ethnic aisle at grocery stores. Filled with fiber and protein, it's a great low-sodium alternative to salt and is terrific in Asian dishes.

Fysh Sauce by Tofuna

Made with tamari, rice vinegar, and seaweed, this commercial product is the answer to traditional fish sauce and is available online and at vegan grocery stores. For a substitute, use 1 teaspoon low-sodium tamari or soy sauce mixed with 1/4 teaspoon dulse flakes for 1 teaspoon Tofuna Fysh Sauce.

Miso Paste

This salty, fermented soybean paste captures the essence of Japanese cooking. It comes in different colors—white, red, and yellow—and some varieties are sweeter than others. It's used extensively in vegan broths, soups, and sauces. Adding miso to foods enhances flavor (see Umami on page 12) and is particularly wonderful on roasted vegetables, where it helps create a delightful glaze. There are soy-free miso brands, as well, using chickpeas, brown rice, and barley. You can find miso in the refrigerated section of grocery stores, usually near the tofu, and there are shelf-stable versions available in some stores in the ethnic or Asian aisle.

Nutritional Yeast

A flaked or powdered condiment, this yeast is grown in a nutrient-rich medium. It gives foods a cheesy, nutty flavor and can create a creamy texture. It's also a favorite among vegans because some brands fortify nutritional yeast with vitamin B_{12}. You can find it in the baking section or bulk section of natural foods stores and some grocery stores.

Nondairy Milk

You'll find milk made from rice, almonds, soybeans, hempseed, and coconut in the refrigerated section of stores and also packaged aseptically. These are usually interchangeable in recipes. However, do not confuse coconut milk sold as a beverage with coconut milk sold in cans. The latter is used in cooking, especially for curried dishes. It's much higher in fat and calories than the type sold as a beverage.

Seitan

Also known as "wheat meat," this glutinous vegan meat is a great protein source. You can find my air fryer version of seitan on page 124. If you have a pressure cooker, I highly suggest you check out the numerous seitan recipes on my website, jlgoesvegan.com. And, great news! Seitan can be found in most grocery stores these days, right next to the tofu. WestSoy and Upton's Naturals are brands that have worked very well in the seitan recipes in this book.

Soy Curls by Butler Foods

Butler Soy Curls are a non-GMO soy food product that uses the whole soybean. Made by Butler Foods, they can be found at most vegan grocery stores, many natural foods stores, and online directly from Butler Foods, Amazon, or veganessentials.com. Since the Soy Curls are dry, the first step is to rehydrate them in warm water or broth (when using them in a traditional chicken recipe, I will rehydrate them in warm chicken-style broth). Add 1 cup Soy Curls to 1 cup warm liquid and allow the curls to sit for 10 minutes. Drain the rehydrated Soy Curls through a colander (and gently squeeze them with tongs). Soy Curls are excellent in stir-fries and salads, and on page 43, you'll see that they also make mighty tasty "fries."

Tempeh

An ancient food from Indonesia, this cake of fermented soybeans has a tender and chewy texture and a savory flavor sometimes described as "yeasty" or "mushroom-like." Tempeh can be made from soybeans only or soybeans in combination with grains. The trick to using tempeh is to steam it before marinating it or cooking it. The steaming process removes some of the bitterness and helps the tempeh absorb the flavors of the recipe. Here's how: Steam the tempeh for 10 minutes in a saucepan on the stove. Alternatively, steam the tempeh for 1 minute on low pressure in an Instant Pot or pressure cooker; use a quick release.

Textured Vegetable Protein (TVP)

Textured vegetable protein (TVP; or textured soy protein [TSP], which is often organic) is a soy food product that, when rehydrated like Butler Soy Curls, is used in the same way as ground meat.

Umami

Umami is a concept in Japanese cooking often referred to as the "fifth flavor." Certain foods and cooking techniques bring out this savory essence, adding a mysterious *wow* to a dish. Such foods include ripe tomatoes, mushrooms (dried and fresh), fermented foods (such as sauerkraut, miso, and soy sauce), wine, nutritional yeast, and more. Cooking techniques include grilling, caramelizing, and roasting—all three of which are included in this book.

Tofu

Made in a similar way to cow's milk cheese, tofu is produced by adding a curdling agent to soy-milk. Throughout Asia, tofu is made fresh daily from soybeans in small shops and sold on the street by vendors. Firm and extra-firm tofu is ideal for tofu steaks and vegetable stir-fries. Soft

tofu is perfect to mash or puree as a filling for sandwiches or lasagna. And the tofu that is traditional to Japanese cooking, silken tofu, is a soft custard-like food that can be blended or pureed for sauces, smoothies, or desserts. On page 103, you'll find my method for foolproof air-fried tofu (hint: you're going to want to freeze it).

Tofu is purchased in blocks packed in water. To use firm or extra-firm tofu in cooking, the water must first be pressed out of it. A manual method of doing so is described in How to Press Tofu on page 13. However, to make this process easier, I suggest purchasing either a TofuXpress or EZ Tofu Press—both which can found at many vegan markets and vegan online stores and Amazon. Simply insert the tofu into either device, press according to the instructions, and your tofu is ready to use!

How to Press Tofu

You'll almost always want to press your firm and extra-firm tofu when air-frying. Here's why and how: Because tofu is packed in water, you want to press and drain it so the spongy soybean block can absorb the flavors of your recipe. Removing the excess liquid also aids in the crunchy exterior you're looking for in fried tofu. Follow these six steps when preparing tofu:

- Open the tofu package and drain out the water.
- Place a clean, lint-free dish towel or paper towels on a baking sheet.
- Put the block of tofu on top of the towels.
- Place a heavy pot on top of the tofu block to press the water out of the tofu.
- Allow the tofu to drain anywhere from 30 minutes to 2 hours.

Now your tofu is ready for a marinade.

Pizza Dough

In addition to the traditional preparation method to make homemade pizza dough, I offer a variation for making it in a bread machine. This dough stores well in the refrigerator for three days—when ready to use, let it warm up to room temperature.

3 3/4 cups all-purpose flour (plus a little more for rolling)
1 1/2 tablespoons sugar
1 1/2 teaspoons active dry yeast
1 1/2 teaspoons salt
1 1/4 cups warm water
4 tablespoons extra-virgin olive oil, divided

In the bowl of a stand mixer, combine the flour, sugar, yeast, and salt. Begin mixing on low and add water, increasing the speed. Add 1 1/3 tablespoons of the oil and mix until the dough forms into a ball. If the dough is a little sticky, add in a little more flour, a small amount at a time, until the dough comes together nicely. If the dough is too dry, add additional water, just a little bit at a time.

Drop the dough onto a lightly floured work surface and gently knead into a smooth, firm ball. Grease a large bowl with 2 teaspoons of the oil, add the dough, and roll it around to coat. Cover the bowl with plastic wrap and put it in a warm area to let it double in size, about 1 hour.

Transfer the dough to a lightly floured work surface. Divide it into two pieces, and roll each into a ball again. Place each ball into an oiled bowl with the remaining oil and cover for 15 to 30 minutes. Once the dough has rested, use it right away or transfer it to a ziplock bag and store in the refrigerator for up to 3 days. If using right away, shape the dough into a pizza pan and let it rest to rise for 10 to 15 minutes. If using refrigerated dough, let it warm up to room temperature before using.

Makes 4 (7-inch) individual pizzas

Variation: To make the dough in a bread machine, add the water, oil, flour, sugar, and salt—in that order—to a bread machine pan. Make a small depression on the top of the flour and add in the yeast. (Don't let the yeast get wet.) Select the "basic dough" setting and press start. When the dough is done, remove from the bread machine pan and drop it onto a lightly floured board. Knead it into a large ball. Divide it into two pieces, and roll each into a ball again. Place each ball into an oiled bowl with the remaining oil and cover for 15 to 30 minutes. Once it's rested, use right away or transfer to a ziplock bag and store in the refrigerator. If using right away, shape the dough into a pizza pan and let it rest to rise for 10 to 15 minutes.

Vegan Broth and Bouillon

Vegetable broth is easy to find in the soup section of any grocery store. These days, you can find chicken- and beef-style vegan broths, bouillon granules or cubes, and even paste to add a layer of flavor to simple recipes (see Umami on page 12). Brands such as Better than Bouillon, Edward & Sons, and Massel can be found near the shelf-stable boxed vegetable broths in many grocery stores. I encourage my coaching clients to keep these on hand when cooking for a "multivore" family (a family in which one or two members may be vegan or vegetarian but others are still eating meat).

Vegetable Broth

Here is my all-time favorite vegetable broth recipe, inspired by a chef friend in New York. You can make it in a pressure cooker (or Instant Pot) in 15 minutes or cook it in a soup pot on the stove in a couple of hours.

1 small peach, quartered
2 small apples, quartered
1 medium onion, quartered
4 cloves garlic, unpeeled and coarsely chopped
8 small carrots, halved
6 celery ribs, halved
1 tomato, quartered
6 whole romaine lettuce leaves
8 cups water
1/2 teaspoon dried oregano
1/2 teaspoon dried sage
1/2 teaspoon dried basil
1/2 teaspoon dried whole rosemary
1 teaspoon sea salt (optional)

Place the peach, apples, onion, garlic, carrots, celery, tomato, lettuce, water, oregano, sage, and basil in a large soup pot or 6-quart or larger pressure cooker (or Instant Pot). Add the rosemary by rubbing it between the palms of your hands into the pot. Add the salt (if using). Stir to combine.

If you are cooking in a soup pot, bring the broth to a boil over high heat, cover, reduce the heat to low, and simmer for 1 1/2 to 2 hours. If you are pressure-cooking, cover the pressure cooker and bring to pressure. Cook at high pressure for 15 minutes. (For a richer broth, cook for 30 minutes.) Remove from the heat and allow for a natural release. Remove the lid from the pressure cooker.

Regardless of the cooking method, after the broth is done, strain it through a fine-mesh strainer or cheesecloth. Use the broth immediately or divide it into portions and refrigerate in airtight glass jars for up to 1 week. You can freeze the broth for up to 6 months in a heavy-duty freezer bag.

Makes 8 to 9 cups of broth

Vegan Cheese

How the times have changed—our vegan cheese cups runneth over! Popular and easily accessible commercial brands include Field Roast's Chao Slices, Daiya, Follow Your Heart, Kite Hill, Miyoko's Creamery, Trader Joe's brand, and Treeline. Many of these cheeses even melt. Sometimes just an ounce will add a kick of flavor to a dish, and in other applications, like the Gourmet Grilled Cheese Sandwich (page 137), you'll want to add more.

Vegan Eggs

Speaking of the times changing, vegan eggs are now a thing. The long-available Ener-G brand egg replacement powder can be found in the baking section in natural grocery stores. The

---

Make Your Own Flax Egg Substitute

If you prefer foods that are less processed, you can make your own vegan egg with ground flaxseed. It's one of the most popular egg substitutes in healthy vegan cooking because it is super easy to make. Makes the equivalent of 1 egg.

1 tablespoon ground flaxseed
3 tablespoons warm water

In a small bowl or measuring cup, combine the flaxseed with the warm water.

Set aside for 10 minutes. After 10 minutes, the mixture should be thickened and ready to use.

Vegg can be found online, and Follow Your Heart's VeganEgg is becoming more and more accessible (it's available on Amazon and veganessentials.com).

For the purposes of air-frying, the VeganEgg is an invaluable ingredient in your kitchen. It's the key to some of the battering and wet-dredging steps in several recipes. It is the only egg replacer that I recommend for the Spinach Omelet (page 28).

DIY "Vegan Magic"

The commercial product Vegan Magic, formerly known as Magic Vegan Bacon Grease, is a coconut oil–based condiment that's great for adding a smoky, bacony flavor to tofu scrambles, vegan omelets, collard greens, and other foods. Vegan Magic can be purchased online and at vegan grocery stores, or you can make your own with this recipe.

1/2 cup coconut oil
1/8 teaspoon paprika
1/8 teaspoon garlic powder
1/8 teaspoon liquid smoke
1/4 teaspoon maple syrup

Combine the oil, paprika, garlic powder, liquid smoke, and maple syrup in a small bowl. Store in an airtight jar at room temperature.

Makes 8 tablespoons

Vegan Butter

There are a number of vegan butters on the market, including Earth Balance, MELT Organic, and Miyoko's Creamery. You can even make your own. I'm a big fan of Bryanna Clark Grogan's recipe, which you can find on her website. Just a dab of it adds flavor to the simplest of recipes.

Worcestershire Sauce

Did you know that traditional Worcestershire sauce is not vegan? One of the ingredients is anchovies. But we live in wonderful times, and vegan versions are now available thanks to the Annie's Homegrown and Edward & Sons brands.

With this background on air-frying and vegan basics, it's time to start cooking.

Let's do this!

3

*B*reakfast can be one of the more challenging meals not only for new vegans but also for any one of us who find ourselves in a morning-meal rut. Air fryer to the rescue! You can now make traditionally nonvegan breakfast items plant-based: sausage, hash browns, and even bacon and eggs. If you have fifteen to thirty minutes to spare in the morning, you're about to start your day off right!

Breakfast and Brunch

Doughnut Holes

I cannot tell you how many people have asked me to create a doughnut recipe for the air fryer. It took some trial and error and, frankly, I didn't like the result. Visually, at least, the doughnuts were not appealing. So I've opted for doughnut holes; they're more fun to cook and eat, anyway. Bonus: they make for a great dessert, too.

2 tablespoons cold nondairy butter
1/2 cup plus 2 tablespoons coconut sugar, divided
1 tablespoon Ener-G brand egg replacer powder or your favorite vegan egg yolk replacement
2 tablespoons water
2 1/4 cups unbleached all-purpose flour
1 1/2 teaspoons baking powder
1 teaspoon salt
1/2 cup plain or vanilla nondairy yogurt
1 to 2 spritzes canola oil
1 teaspoon ground cinnamon

In a large bowl, combine the butter and 1/2 cup of the sugar and mix well, using your hands until clumps form.

In a small bowl or cup, whisk the egg replacer with the water. Add it to the butter and sugar and mix well. Set aside.

In a medium bowl, combine the flour, baking powder, and salt.

Add the flour mixture to the butter mixture and mix well. Fold in the yogurt. Mix until a dough is formed.

Roll pieces of dough into 18 (1-inch) balls and arrange them on a large baking sheet or piece of parchment paper.

Grease the air fryer with the oil. Preheat the air fryer to 360°F for 3 minutes. Transfer the doughnut holes to the air fryer basket. Cook for 8 minutes, shaking halfway through the cooking time.

Mix the remaining 2 tablespoons sugar and cinnamon on a plate. Roll the hot doughnut holes lightly in the cinnamon sugar before transferring them to a baking rack to cool.

Makes 18 doughnut holes

Basic Breakfast Potatoes

Okay, I know the point of this book is that you can make all kinds of things in the air fryer, not just potatoes. But, come on, you know you were interested in crispy, low- to no-oil fried potatoes!

> 2 large red or russet potatoes, scrubbed
> 1 small yellow onion, cut into half-moon slices (cut the onion in half lengthwise, and then slice along the lines of the onion)
> 1 teaspoon extra-virgin olive oil or canola oil
> 1/2 teaspoon sea salt (optional)
> 1/4 teaspoon black pepper

Preheat the air fryer to 360°F for 3 minutes. Shred the potatoes in a food processor or with a cheese grater using the big holes.

Transfer the shredded potatoes and onion to a medium bowl. Add the oil, salt (if using), and pepper. Toss with tongs to coat.

Transfer to the air fryer basket. Cook for 12 to 15 minutes, or until golden brown, shaking every 3 minutes. Serve hot.

Serves 4

No-Oil Option: Omit the olive oil and use parchment paper or foil to avoid sticking.

NOTE

This recipe does especially well on a grill accessory.

Tempeh and Veggie Scramble-ish

Tofu scramble is a morning vegan staple. This air-fried tempeh version departs from the traditional tofu sauté. Try this over steamed kale or collard greens and serve with diced avocado.

8 ounces tempeh
2 cloves garlic, minced
1 teaspoon ground turmeric
1 teaspoon ground cumin
1/2 teaspoon chili powder
1/2 teaspoon black salt
1/4 to 1/2 cup low-sodium vegetable broth
1 to 2 spritzes extra-virgin olive oil
1 cup coarsely chopped cremini mushrooms (or your favorite mushroom)
1 small red onion, quartered
1/2 cup coarsely chopped bell pepper (any color)
1/2 cup sliced cherry or grape tomatoes

Steam the tempeh for 10 minutes (see page 12). (This step is optional, but I'm a huge fan of steaming tempeh in advance to help it absorb marinade, tame its bitterness, and soften its texture a bit.) Cut the tempeh into 12 equal cubes.

In a shallow bowl, combine the garlic, turmeric, cumin, chili powder, black salt, and broth. Add the steamed tempeh and marinate for a minimum of 30 minutes or up to overnight.

Spray the air fryer basket with the oil (alternatively, wipe the basket with oil). Drain the tempeh and add it to the air fryer basket. Add the mushrooms, onion, and bell pepper.

Cook at 330°F for 10 minutes. Add the tomatoes, increase the heat to 390°F, and cook 3 more minutes.

Serves 4

No-Oil Option: Omit the olive oil and shake frequently to avoid sticking.

Tofu Bacon Wraps

The current darling of the Internet, rice paper bacon, just got amped up here because we're upping the protein game. I decided to try this by wrapping thin tofu slices in rice paper—the result is a crunchy exterior and meaty interior. Rice paper is the wrap used in spring rolls. You can find it at Asian markets, in the ethnic aisle of many grocery stores, and online.

8 ounces extra-firm tofu, drained and pressed (page 13)
4 (6 to 8 1/2-inch) sheets rice paper
2 tablespoons maple syrup
1 teaspoon avocado oil or extra-virgin olive oil
1/2 teaspoon vegan Worcestershire sauce, tamari, or soy sauce
1/8 teaspoon liquid smoke
1/2 teaspoon cayenne pepper

Cut the tofu lengthwise into 8 slices and set aside. Cut the rice paper sheets in half for a total of 8 pieces.

In a small bowl, combine the maple syrup, oil, Worcestershire sauce, liquid smoke, and cayenne to create a marinade.

Dip a piece of the rice paper in warm water for about 5 seconds or until it's moistened. Place the moist rice paper on a cutting board and let sit for 30 seconds or until it's pliable.

Place a piece of tofu on a half-sheet of rice paper. Brush the marinade over the tofu and the rice paper. Roll the tofu into the wrapper, rolling away from you, and fold, closing the ends of the wrapper toward the tofu (it's pliable and will easily stick). Brush marinade on both sides of the bacon. Repeat this process with the remaining tofu and rice paper.

Transfer the wrapped tofu to the air fryer basket. Cook at 360°F for 6 minutes. Increase the heat to 390°F and cook 2 minutes longer.

Makes 8 pieces

Breakfast (Pan)Cake

If we fry up pancakes in a skillet, then why not in an air fryer? The trick here is finding the right accessory. An 8-inch springform pan works great in a large air fryer. Pour all the batter in the pan and bake it like a cake. But don't be selfish—this recipe is for two, so share! If you have a smaller device, find a smaller, heatproof dish and use less batter. You may have to make one pancake and then another; if so, put the prepared pancake on a plate in a warm oven while the other cooks.

    1/2 cup unbleached all-purpose flour
    2 tablespoons coconut sugar or granulated sugar
    1 tablespoon baking powder
    1 to 2 pinches sea salt
    1/2 cup soymilk or other nondairy milk
    1 tablespoon applesauce
    1/4 teaspoon vanilla extract
    1 to 2 spritzes extra-virgin olive oil spray

Combine the flour, sugar, baking powder, and salt in a mixing bowl. Slowly whisk in the milk, applesauce, and vanilla extract.

Preheat the air fryer to 330°F for 3 minutes. Grease an 8-inch springform pan (or an oven-safe dish of your choice) with the olive oil spray.

Pour the batter into the prepared pan. Cook at 330°F for 10 minutes. Check for doneness by inserting a toothpick into the center—it should come out dry. Cook for an additional 2 to 4 minutes as needed.

Serves 2

No-Oil Option: Omit the olive oil and layer the baking pan with parchment paper (no paper should be exposed).

NOTE

Double or triple this recipe and keep the batter in an airtight container (a mason jar is great) in the refrigerator. You'll be all set to make it again the next day!

Fried Biscuits

My husband, Dave, gets all the credit for this recipe. He loves a biscuit sandwich and came up with a simple recipe that cooks up beautifully in the air fryer! This is a perfect example of how two people who, at the time, followed different diets (I was vegan; he, not so much) would create recipes that were pleasing to both. I truly believe that the collaboration helped move Dave along his journey to becoming a vegan. (See photo of Fried Biscuits on page 32.) This recipe can easily be doubled, but note that you'll need to air-fry the biscuits in two batches.

1/2 cup almond milk
1 1/2 teaspoons fresh lemon juice
1 cup unbleached all-purpose flour
1 1/2 teaspoons baking powder
1/4 teaspoon baking soda
1/2 teaspoon sea salt
2 tablespoons plus 2 teaspoons cold nondairy butter

In a small bowl, combine the milk and lemon juice and refrigerate for 10 minutes.

In large bowl, combine the flour, baking powder, baking soda, and salt, and mix well. Use a knife to cut the butter into small pieces in the bowl and then break them up into the flour mixture. To avoid melting the butter, quickly mix the butter and flour together—don't be afraid to use your hands. Continue mixing until the mixture resembles bread crumbs. Add the chilled milk mixture and combine with a wooden spoon until a dough has formed.

Transfer the dough to a floured work surface. Dust the top of the dough with additional flour and fold and press it 5 or 6 times, until you achieve a circle of dough about 1 inch thick. Use a biscuit cutter or circular mold to cut out 4 biscuits from the dough. Do this by pressing straight down through the dough. Place the biscuits close in the air fryer basket, so that they are barely touching. Continue to re-form the remaining dough to make additional biscuits. Do this quickly as overhandling the dough could impact how the biscuits rise.

Preheat the air fryer to 400°F for 5 minutes. Add the biscuits and cook for 7 minutes, until golden brown.

Makes 4 biscuits

Spinach Omelet

The times have changed and so have our vegan egg options. Although I provide a couple of vegan egg options in chapter 2 (page 16), this recipe really only works with the Follow Your Heart VeganEgg product. You just can't beat the fluffy result. I also use Vegan Magic—formerly known as Magic Vegan Bacon Grease—to add a smoky flavor.

1 cup ice cold water
4 tablespoons Follow Your Heart VeganEgg
2 tablespoons chickpea flour
1/4 teaspoon black salt
1 teaspoon Vegan Magic or DIY "Vegan Magic" (page 17)
1/2 cup finely chopped red bell pepper
1/2 cup finely chopped yellow onion
Freshly ground black pepper
2 cups loosely packed baby spinach

Combine the water, VeganEgg, flour, and salt in the blender and blend until smooth. Set aside.

Add the Vegan Magic to a baking pan that will fit into your air fryer. Place the baking pan in the air fryer and preheat to 390°F for 3 minutes.

Pour the omelet mixture into the baking pan and cook for 2 minutes at 390°F. Add the bell pepper and onion, patting them into the omelet mixture, and cook for 3 minutes longer.

Pause the machine to add the pepper and spinach to the omelet. Fold the omelet in half and cook for 5 more minutes at 390°F. Cut into 2 servings.

Serves 2

No-Oil Option: Omit the Vegan Magic.

Tempeh Bacon

Sure, you can buy vegan bacon—and there are some terrific options—but why not turn to tempeh, a traditional Indonesian food, for a heartier version? The chewy texture holds up well in an air fryer. (See photo on page 36.)

8 ounces tempeh
2 tablespoons maple syrup
1 teaspoon avocado oil or extra-virgin olive oil
1/2 teaspoon vegan Worcestershire sauce, tamari, or soy sauce
1/8 teaspoon liquid smoke
1/2 teaspoon cayenne pepper

Steam the tempeh for 10 minutes. (This step is optional, but to see why I recommend it, refer to page 12.) Transfer the tempeh to a shallow bowl.

In a small bowl, combine the maple syrup, oil, Worcestershire sauce, liquid smoke, and cayenne, whisking until well blended. Pour the marinade over the tempeh and marinate for at least 1 hour (overnight is better).

Place the tempeh slices in the air fryer basket. Cook for 10 minutes at 330°F. Shake after 5 minutes. Increase the heat to 390°F and cook for 3 minutes longer.

Makes 8 pieces

No-Oil Option: Omit the avocado oil.

Miso-Style Vegetables

In 2011, I accidentally took a three-day macrobiotic cooking class in Philadelphia (long story). I learned some great cooking techniques and, of course, picked up on how wonderful Japanese-style savory porridge and braised vegetables are for breakfast. (Break out of that cereal rut, folks!) These umami-packed vegetables are wonderful on their own or served over a savory porridge.

1 tablespoon white miso
2 tablespoons soy sauce
2 tablespoons rice vinegar
1 teaspoon sesame oil (optional)
2 cups finely chopped carrots
2 cups broccoli florets
1/2 cup finely chopped daikon radish

In a small bowl, combine the miso, soy sauce, vinegar, and sesame oil (if using). Mix well.

In a large mixing bowl, combine the carrots, broccoli, and daikon. Pour the miso mixture over the vegetables and toss with tongs to coat completely. Preheat the air fryer to 330°F for 5 minutes.

Transfer the vegetables to the air fryer basket and cook for 25 minutes, shaking every 5 minutes.

Serves 4

Variation: Try this with all kinds of vegetables!

Low-Oil Option: Opt for a quick spritz of sesame oil.

No-Oil Option: Omit the sesame oil.

Bacon and Egg Sandwiches

In this book, we've got two kinds of bacon (pages 25 and 30). We've got biscuits (page 27). It seems like it's time for a vegan bacon and egg breakfast, yes? The egg, in this case, is tofu, so feel free to use a store-bought bacon if you'd rather not load up on soy.

1 (16-ounce) package extra-firm tofu
1/2 cup soymilk
1/4 cup plus 2 tablespoons nutritional yeast
2 teaspoons ground turmeric
1 teaspoon garlic powder
1/2 teaspoon black salt
3 tablespoons unbleached all-purpose flour
1 tablespoon potato starch
2 to 4 spritzes canola oil spray
4 strips Tempeh Bacon (page 30) or store-bought vegan bacon
4 Fried Biscuits (page 27) or store-bought vegan biscuits

Drain and press the tofu (see the sidebar on page 13 for instructions). Cut the tofu into 4 equal pieces. Then cut each piece in half, for a total of 8 slices.

In a small bowl, whisk together the milk, nutritional yeast, turmeric, garlic powder, and black salt until combined. Set aside.

Mix the flour and potato starch together on a large plate for dredging. Dip each piece of tofu in the milk mixture. Then lightly coat each piece with the flour mixture.

Spray the air fryer basket with the canola oil. Place the coated pieces of tofu in the basket and lightly spray the top of the tofu. Cook at 360°F for 6 minutes. Flip the tofu slices and cook for 6 minutes longer. Place two tofu eggs and one piece of vegan bacon on each biscuit.

Serves 4

Variation: Use the Spinach Omelet (page 28) as an alternative to the tofu eggs.

No-Oil Option: Start with parchment paper or foil for the first 5 minutes of cooking. Be careful to very lightly coat the tofu pieces with the flour and starch mixture, you may end up with white blotches of flour instead of an even golden-brown exterior.

Breakfast and Brunch

Sausage-Style Soy Curl Hash

Soy Curls are much like tofu, as they grab the flavors of the spices and seasonings you use—in this case, a fragrant meaty dish (that's also full of compassion). You can find additional information about Soy Curls on page 11. I love using them in recipes because they are made from whole soybeans and they add a meaty texture to any meal.

2 cups dry Soy Curls
2 cups warm water
2 small potatoes, cut into 1/4-inch cubes
1/4 teaspoon sea salt
1/4 teaspoon black pepper
2 teaspoons vegan beef bouillon granules
1 teaspoon dried sage
1/2 teaspoon ground ginger
1/2 teaspoon cayenne pepper
1/4 teaspoon anise seeds or fennel seeds, crushed
1 teaspoon extra-virgin olive oil
2 tablespoons maple syrup
1 small onion, cut into 1/8-inch thick half-moon slices

Combine the dry Soy Curls and the warm water in a large bowl to rehydrate. Set aside. Toss the potatoes with the salt and pepper and transfer them to the air fryer. Cook for 10 minutes at 400°F. While the potatoes are cooking, drain the Soy Curls and return them to the bowl. Add the bouillon granules, sage, ginger, cayenne, anise seeds, oil, maple syrup, and onion. Toss well, until the Soy Curls are completely coated.

Add the Soy Curls to the air fryer once the potatoes have cooked for the 10 minutes. Shake the basket to distribute the ingredients or use tongs to toss. Cook the potatoes and Soy Curls for 20 minutes longer, shaking halfway through the cooking time.

Serves 4

No-Oil Option: Omit the olive oil.

Slider and Bacon Bloody Marys

This had to happen. See, there's this tavern in my town making a mean Blood Mary every Sunday, and it's such a sight to behold. But it's not even close to vegan. Less of a recipe and more of a "pull this all together yourself" technique, here's my version.

2 (1/2-inch thick) slices Gimme Lean Sausage or Baked Chick'n-Style Seitan (page 124)
2 slices Tempeh Bacon (page 30) or store-bought vegan bacon
6 to 8 ounces vegan Bloody Mary mix
2 to 4 ounces vodka (optional)
2 ribs celery
2 vegan slider buns
2 to 4 pitted green olives or lime wedges (optional)
2 sweet or dill pickle slices or cherry tomatoes (optional)

Place the sausage slices in the air fryer basket. Add the bacon. Cook at 370°F for 6 minutes.

Use the Bloody Mary mix and vodka (if using) to mix your favorite adult or virgin Bloody Mary. Be sure to use a glass that holds at least 12 ounces of liquid (a mason jar is a fun option). Add a rib of celery to each drink.

Assemble the cooked sausages on the slider buns and pierce them with a skewer. If using the olives and pickles, add them to the skewers, too. Place the skewers in each drink, propping them on the edges of the glasses. Add a cooked bacon strip to each Bloody Mary.

Serves 2

4

*B*efore I purchased my air fryer, serving an appetizer was something I did only when entertaining. Now I can toss some food into the air fryer, make a quick bite, and we can snack while cooking dinner. Having said that, I've been known to serve many of these recipes as meals: Soy Curl Fries (page 43) add bulk and texture to an ordinary salad. Fried Tofu with Peanut Sauce (page 59) over a bed of rice can make a perfect main dish.

Starters and Snacks

Vegetable Egg Rolls

Egg rolls—don't sound very vegan, do they? Surprisingly, vegetable egg rolls at restaurants actually can be vegan, because the wrappers do not contain egg. But finding egg-free wrappers at mainstream grocery stores can be challenging. I buy my vegan spring and egg roll wrappers at our local Asian market, so look for an Asian market near you.

  1 to 2 teaspoons canola oil
  1 cup shredded cabbage
  1 cup grated carrots
  1 cup bean sprouts
  1/2 cup finely chopped mushrooms (any type)
  1/2 cup sliced scallions
  2 teaspoons chili paste
  1/2 teaspoon ground ginger
  1/4 cup low-sodium soy sauce or tamari
  2 teaspoons potato starch
  8 vegan egg roll wrappers

In a large skillet, heat the oil over medium-high heat. Add the cabbage, carrots, bean sprouts, mushrooms, scallions, chili paste, and ginger. Sauté for 3 minutes.

In a small bowl or measuring cup, whisk together the soy sauce and potato starch. Pour this mixture into the skillet and combine with the vegetables.

Lay the egg roll wrappers out on a work surface. Lightly brush the edges with water. Place 1/4 cup of the filling at one end of the wrapper. Begin rolling the wrapper over the vegetables, tucking in the ends after the first roll. Repeat this process with the remaining wrappers and filling.

Transfer the egg rolls to the air fryer basket. Cook at 360°F for 6 minutes, shaking halfway through the cooking time.

Makes 8 eggrolls

No-Oil Option: Use vegetable broth instead of canola oil or dry-sauté the vegetables.

Barbecue Potato Chips

Sure, I could have written a plain old potato chip recipe, but this is a cookbook, and your expectations should be higher! Barbecue chips are one of my favorites, but most store brands contain milk or other nonvegan products. Though the ingredient list in this vegan version is long, don't let that intimidate you. I bet you have most of the ingredients in your spice rack right now. (See chips in the photo on page 114.) P.S. I won't be offended if you skip all the spices and just make straight-up chips.

1 large russet potato
1 teaspoon paprika
1/2 teaspoon garlic salt
1/4 teaspoon sugar
1/4 teaspoon onion powder
1/4 teaspoon chipotle powder or chili powder
1/8 teaspoon sea salt
1/8 teaspoon ground mustard
1/8 teaspoon cayenne pepper
1 teaspoon canola oil
1/8 teaspoon liquid smoke

Wash and peel the potato. Cut into thin, 1/10-inch slices; consider using a mandolin slicer or the slicer blade in a food processor to achieve consistent slices.

Fill a large bowl with 3 to 4 cups very cold water. Transfer the potato slices to the bowl and soak them for 20 minutes.

In a small bowl, combine the paprika, garlic salt, sugar, onion powder, chipotle powder, sea salt, mustard, and cayenne.

Rinse and drain the potato slices and pat them dry with a paper towel. Transfer them to a large bowl. Add the oil, liquid smoke, and spice mixture to the bowl. Toss to coat. Transfer the potatoes to the air fryer basket.

Cook at 390°F for 20 minutes. Shake every 5 minutes to keep an eye on the progress. You want brown, but not burnt, chips. Eat these right away!

Serves 4

No-Oil Option: Omit the canola oil.

Soy Curl Fries

I suspect you'll be cooking a lot of potatoes in your air fryer. Here's an alternative fry that is great for snacking but could easily serve as an entrée. Chop these fries and serve them as a topping on a salad or roll them up in a tortilla with raw veggies and nondairy mayo for a quick sandwich wrap.

> 1 cup dry Soy Curls
> 1 cup hot vegan chicken broth
> 1/2 teaspoon chili powder
> 1 teaspoon brown rice flour
> 1 teaspoon cornstarch
> 1 teaspoon chipotle avocado oil (or plain avocado oil plus 1/2 teaspoon chipotle powder)

Rehydrate the Soy Curls in the hot broth for 10 minutes. Drain the Soy Curls and gently press them with tongs to remove the excess liquid.

Transfer the drained Soy Curls to a large bowl. Add the chili powder, flour, cornstarch, and oil. Toss until well coated.

Transfer the Soy Curls to the air fryer and cook at 390°F for 8 minutes, shaking halfway through the cooking time.

Serves 2

No-Oil Option: Omit the avocado oil and use 1 tablespoon vegetable broth.

Seasoned French Fries

These tasty spuds are a great alternative to plain fries. You can have so much fun with the spices and seasonings. Use curry for an Indian-inspired snack or parsley and oregano for a taste of Italy.

> 2 large russet potatoes, scrubbed
> 1 tablespoon avocado oil or extra-virgin olive oil
> 1 teaspoon dried dill
> 1 teaspoon dried chives
> 1 teaspoon dried parsley
> 1 teaspoon cayenne pepper
> 2 tablespoons chickpea, soy, buckwheat, or millet flour

Cut the potatoes into 1/4-inch slices, then cut the slices into 1/4-inch strips. Transfer the fries to a large bowl and cover them in 3 to 4 cups water. Soak the fries for 20 minutes. Drain, rinse, and pat dry.

Return the potatoes to the bowl. Add the avocado oil, dill, chives, parsley, cayenne, and flour. Toss until well coated.

Preheat the air fryer to 390°F for 3 minutes. Transfer the coated potatoes to the air fryer basket. Cook for 20 minutes, shaking halfway through the cooking time.

Serves 2 to 4

No-Oil Option: Omit the avocado oil.

Jalapeño Poppers

All the credit for this recipe goes to my husband. Don't get me wrong, I wanted to make these, but it was Dave who reached back into his way-back, pre-vegan food memories, and this simple and delectable recipe was born.

8 large jalapeños
1 cup nondairy cream cheese
1/4 cup finely chopped onion
1 cup unseasoned dry bread crumbs
2 teaspoons dried Mexican oregano
1/2 teaspoon freshly ground black pepper
1/2 to 1 teaspoon salt, or to taste
2 to 3 spritzes extra-virgin olive oil

When preparing the jalapeños, consider wearing latex gloves to avoid irritating your skin. Cut the jalapeños in half lengthwise, following the curve of the peppers. With a small spoon or your fingers, scoop out the seeds and the membrane, as they contain the heat of the jalapeños (leave a few seeds if you want extra heat). Set the sliced jalapeños aside.

In a small bowl, mix together the cream cheese and onion.

In a medium bowl, combine the bread crumbs, Mexican oregano, pepper, and salt.

Fill each jalapeño half with approximately 2 teaspoons of the cream cheese mixture, pressing it into the cavity with your fingers. Sprinkle 1 1/2 teaspoons of the bread crumb mixture over the cream cheese. Press the bread crumbs into the cream cheese.

Spritz the air fryer basket with the oil. Place as many jalapeño poppers into the air fryer basket as will fit (you may have to cook in batches). Spritz the top of the poppers with additional oil (this will help them brown). Cook at 390°F for 6 to 7 minutes, or until the bread crumbs are golden brown.

Serves 4 to 6

No-Oil Option: Omit the olive oil (but note that the final result may not be golden brown).

Spicy Mac 'n' Cheese Balls

I'm not supposed to have favorites in this book, but c'mon! The title sounds like the opposite of healthy, but take a long, hard look at the ingredient list: it is mostly whole foods with a wee bit of nondairy cheese. For a real treat, dip these into a simple warmed marinara sauce with a pinch of red pepper flakes.

2 3/4 cups vegan chicken broth, divided
1 cup whole-wheat fusilli
1 tablespoon nondairy butter
2 cloves garlic, minced
1/4 cup finely chopped yellow onion
1/4 cup plus 1 tablespoon chickpea flour, divided
1/4 cup nutritional yeast
1 teaspoon fresh lemon juice
1/4 cup nondairy shredded Daiya Jalapeño Havarti Style Farmhouse Block or Pepperjack
    Style cheese
1/4 teaspoon black pepper
2 flax eggs (page 16) or 2 tablespoons Follow Your Heart VeganEgg or Ener-G Egg Replacer
1/2 cup ice cold water
1/2 cup dry Italian bread crumbs
1 teaspoon smoked paprika
1 teaspoon cayenne pepper
1/4 cup nondairy shredded Parmesan cheese
3 to 4 spritzes extra-virgin olive oil

In a large saucepan, bring 2 1/2 cups of the broth to a boil over medium-high heat. Add the fusilli and cook for 11 minutes.

In a small saucepan, heat the butter, garlic, and onion over medium-low heat. Once the butter is boiling, reduce the heat to low and simmer for 5 minutes.

Add 1 tablespoon of the chickpea flour to the butter and whisk to make a roux.

Drain the cooked fusilli and return it to the large saucepan. Transfer the roux to the pasta and stir in the nutritional yeast, lemon juice, and cheese. Add as much of the remaining 1/4 cup broth as necessary for a creamy consistency. Transfer the fusilli to a large bowl, cover, and refrigerate for 1 to 2 hours.

Set up 3 dredging stations. Pour the remaining 1/4 cup of chickpea flour in a shallow bowl. Combine the flax eggs and cold water in a second shallow bowl. Combine the bread crumbs, smoked paprika, cayenne, and Parmesan in a third shallow bowl. Preheat the air fryer to 390°F for 3 minutes.

Scoop out 2 tablespoons of the chilled mac 'n' cheese and roll into a ball until you have made 8 balls. Roll each ball in the chickpea flour (shaking each one to remove excess flour), then dip the ball into the flax egg, and finally coat the ball with the bread crumb mixture. Set each one aside on a plate or piece of parchment paper until all 8 mac 'n' cheese balls are prepared.

Transfer the balls to the air fryer basket and spritz them with the oil. Cook for 8 minutes or until golden brown.

Makes 8 mac 'n' cheese balls

Fried Vegetable Wontons

Here's another great starter for your next Asian meal. Though, with the use of tofu, might I suggest dumplings for dinner?

1/4 cup finely chopped carrots
1/4 cup finely chopped extra-firm tofu
1/4 cup finely chopped shiitake mushrooms
1/2 cup finely chopped cabbage
1 tablespoon minced garlic
1 teaspoon dried ground ginger
1/4 teaspoon white pepper
2 teaspoons soy sauce, divided
1 teaspoon sesame oil
2 teaspoons potato starch or cornstarch
16 vegan wonton wrappers
1 to 2 spritzes canola oil or extra-virgin olive oil
Spicy Soy Dipping Sauce (follows)

In a large bowl, combine the carrots, tofu, mushrooms, cabbage, garlic, ginger, white pepper, and 1 teaspoon of the soy sauce.

In a small bowl, combine the remaining 1 teaspoon soy sauce, sesame oil, and potato starch. Whisk until the starch is completely combined. Pour over the tofu and vegetables and combine well using your hands.

Set a small bowl of water next to your work surface to make the dumplings. Lay a wonton wrapper flat, wet the sides with water using your finger, and place 1 tablespoon of the filling in the center. Pull all 4 corners of the wrapper up to the top and center and pinch them together. Set the wontons in the air fryer basket. Repeat this process, making a total of 16 wontons. Spritz the wontons with the canola oil. Cook at 360°F for 6 minutes, shaking halfway through the cooking time.

Transfer the fried wontons to a plate and serve with the dipping sauce.

Makes 16 wontons

Low-Oil Option: Omit the canola oil.

Spicy Soy Dipping Sauce

1 tablespoon low-sodium soy sauce
1 teaspoon rice vinegar
1/2 teaspoon chili paste

In a small bowl, combine the soy sauce, vinegar, and chili paste.

Makes 1 1/3 tablespoons

Szekely Goulash Pastry Bites

In my cookbook, *Vegan Pressure Cooking,* I created a chickpea version of a traditional Hungarian dish that my husband ate at family gatherings while growing up. This time around, Dave was an active participant (okay, creator), and his seitan version of New World Hungarian makes for a clever little appetizer.

2 teaspoons extra-virgin olive oil or canola oil
4 ounces Baked Chick'n-Style Seitan (page 124) or store-bought seitan, cut into 1/4-inch cubes
1/2 cup finely chopped onion
1 clove garlic, minced
1/4 to 1/2 teaspoon salt, to taste
1/4 teaspoon ground black pepper, or more to taste
1/2 teaspoon ground cumin
2 teaspoons paprika, divided
8 ounces sauerkraut, drained well
1/2 cup nondairy sour cream, divided
Unbleached all-purpose flour, as needed
8 uncooked vegan crescent rolls

In a medium saucepan, heat the oil over medium heat. Once the oil is hot, add the seitan, stirring to coat it in the oil. Add the onion, garlic, salt, pepper, cumin, and 1 1/2 teaspoons of the paprika. Sauté for 3 to 5 minutes, until the onion is translucent.

Add the sauerkraut and stir gently to incorporate. Cook for 5 minutes longer. Add 1/4 cup of the sour cream, stirring well, and cook for 3 to 5 minutes. Preheat the air fryer to 360°F for 4 minutes.

Sprinkle a work surface with flour. Place a crescent roll triangle on the prepared surface and shape the dough into a square. Roll the dough with a floured rolling pin to achieve a thin, 4-inch square.

Spoon 1/4 cup goulash into the middle of the pastry square. Fold by bringing each corner to the center and pinch them together to form a tuft on top. Repeat this process to form 8 pastry bites.

Transfer the pastry bites to the air fryer basket. Cook at 360°F for 5 minutes, until golden brown.

Add the remaining 1/4 cup sour cream to a dipping bowl. Sprinkle with the remaining 1/2 teaspoon paprika.

Using tongs, remove the pastry bites from the air basket gently, as there may be some sticking, and place them on a plate. Serve the bites with the sour cream (and a fork and knife).

Serves 4 (makes 8 bites)

No-Oil Option: Omit the olive oil.

Fried Avocado

I first made these as an appetizer for a big Mexican feast. But they are also great as a filling for tacos—simply place the fried avocado in a warm corn tortilla and garnish with finely diced tomatoes, fresh cilantro, and a wedge of lime to squeeze over the taco.

> 1/4 cup unbleached all-purpose flour
> 1 Flax Egg (page 16)
> 1/2 cup panko bread crumbs
> 1 teaspoon chili powder
> 1 ripe Hass avocado, pitted and peeled
> 2 to 3 spritzes canola oil or extra-virgin olive oil

Place the flour in a shallow dish. Place the flax egg in a second shallow dish. In a third shallow dish, combine the panko bread crumbs and chili powder.

Dredge each avocado half through the three coating stations: cover it in flour, dip it in the flax egg, and coat it with the panko bread crumbs.

Spritz the air fryer basket with the oil. Place the coated avocado halves in a single layer in the air fryer basket. Spritz the avocado halves with oil. Cook at 390°F for 12 minutes.

Serves 2

No-Oil Option: Omit the canola oil.

Beany Jackfruit Taquitos

Taquitos (or flautas) are essentially rolled corn-tortilla tacos that are fried. While taquitos are traditionally filled with beef or chicken, this vegan version uses jackfruit, an odd plant-based ingredient that gets stringy and meaty when cooked. The addition of beans to the jackfruit boosts protein content and satiety.

1 (14-ounce) can water-packed jackfruit, drained and rinsed
1 cup cooked or canned red beans, drained and rinsed
1/2 cup pico de gallo sauce
1/4 cup plus 2 tablespoons water
4 (6-inch) corn or whole wheat tortillas
2 to 4 spritzes canola oil or extra-virgin olive oil

In a medium saucepan or pressure cooker, combine the jackfruit, beans, pico de gallo, and water. If you are using a saucepan, heat the jackfruit mixture over medium-high heat until it begins to boil. Reduce the heat, cover the saucepan, and simmer for 20 to 25 minutes. If you are using a pressure cooker, cover the pressure cooker, bring to pressure, cook at low pressure for 3 minutes, and then use a natural release.

Mash the jackfruit mixture with a fork or potato masher. You're aiming to shred the jackfruit to a meaty texture. Preheat the air fryer to 370°F for 3 minutes.

Place a tortilla on a work surface. Spoon 1/4 cup of the jackfruit mixture onto the tortilla. Roll it up tightly, pushing any of the mixture that falls out back into the tortilla. Repeat this process to make 4 taquitos.

Spritz the air fryer basket with the oil. Spritz the tops of the tortillas as well. Place the rolled tortillas into the air fryer basket. Cook at 370°F for 8 minutes.

Makes 4 taquitos

No-Oil Option: Omit the canola oil.

Air-Fried Pretzels

This recipe requires a bit more work than some of the others, but it's worth it! Serve these pretzels piping hot with a hearty, whole-grain brown mustard. Or take a look at the variations below. You can use this same recipe to make forty pretzel bites or six super special hot dog buns!

3/4 cup warm water (110 to 115°F)
1 teaspoon instant yeast
1/2 teaspoon salt
2 teaspoons granulated sugar
1 1/2 cups unbleached all-purpose flour, divided, plus more as needed
4 1/2 cups water
1/4 cup baking soda
1 1/4 teaspoons coarse sea salt

Whisk together the warm water and yeast in a large measuring cup. Add the salt and sugar and stir until combined.

In a medium mixing bowl, combine 1 cup of the flour with the yeast mixture, stirring with a wooden spoon. Add another 1/4 cup flour, stirring until the dough is no longer sticky and is easy to handle.

Scatter the remaining 1/4 cup flour on a work surface. Transfer the dough to the work surface and knead it for 3 to 4 minutes. Add more flour if the dough sticks to the work surface or your hands.

After kneading the dough, shape it into a 5 x 5 x 1/2-inch square.

In a large pot over medium-high heat, bring the water and baking soda to a boil.

Meanwhile, cut the block of dough lengthwise into 5 strips.

Roll each strip out into 12-inch ropes. Take both ends of a rope, draw them together, and make a full twist, using your hands to shape a circle with the dough still on the work surface. Press the ends of the dough into the circle, forming the iconic pretzel shape. Repeat this process with the remaining ropes, making 5 pretzels.

Place 1 pretzel on a slotted spoon and place it gently into the boiling water. It will sink and then float to the top in about 20 to 30 seconds. Remove the pretzel with a slotted spoon and transfer to it a silicone baking mat or piece of parchment paper.

Repeat this process with the remaining 4 pretzels.

Preheat the air fryer to 390°F for 5 minutes. Sprinkle 1/4 teaspoon salt on each pretzel.

Transfer the pretzels to the air fryer basket. If using a large air fryer with a rack accessory, you can place 2 larger pretzels directly on the basket and 3 smaller on the rack. If you are using a smaller air fryer or if there is no rack available, fry the pretzels in batches.

Cook at 390°F for 5 to 6 minutes. Begin checking on them at 3 minutes. You're looking for a golden to dark brown result. Remove the pretzels from the air fryer with a spatula.

Makes 5 pretzels

Variations

Pretzel Bites: Follow the preceding instructions for pretzels but instead of forming the dough into pretzels, cut each of the 5 ropes into 1-inch bites.

Makes about 40 pretzel bites

Pretzel Hot Dog Buns: Follow the preceding instructions for pretzels. Once you have kneaded the dough for 3 to 4 minutes, shape the dough into a 6 x 5-inch rectangle. Cut the dough lengthwise into 6 pieces. Shape each piece into a 5-inch long bun.

In a large pot over medium-high heat, bring the water and baking soda to a boil. Gently place 2 buns at a time into the boiling water. The buns will sink and then float to the top in about 30 seconds. Remove the buns with a large slotted spoon and transfer them to a piece of parchment paper. Repeat this process with the remaining buns.

Preheat the air fryer to 390°F for 5 minutes. Transfer the pretzel buns to the air fryer basket. If using a large air fryer with a rack accessory, you can place 3 buns directly on the basket and 3 on the rack. If you are using a smaller air fryer or if no rack is available, fry the hot dog buns in batches. Cook at 390°F for 6 to 7 minutes, until the buns turn golden to dark brown. Remove the buns from the air fryer with a spatula.

Let the buns cool for 10 minutes before slicing lengthwise along their tops.

Makes 6 hot dog buns

Fried Tofu with Peanut Sauce

When I dine out at Asian restaurants, I often want to order the tofu appetizer but find it either bland or not vegan (bonito flakes are often used). Here's the crispy tofu appetizer I dream of.

Fried Tofu
1 (12-ounce) package firm tofu, drained and pressed (page 13)
1/2 cup cornmeal
1/4 cup cornstarch
1/2 teaspoon sea salt
1/2 teaspoon white pepper
1/2 teaspoon red pepper flakes
1 to 2 spritzes sesame oil

Peanut Sauce
1 (1-inch) piece fresh ginger, peeled
1 clove garlic
1/2 cup creamy peanut butter
2 tablespoons low-sodium tamari
1 tablespoon fresh lime juice
1 teaspoon maple syrup
1/2 teaspoon chili paste
1/4 to 1/2 cup water, as needed
1/4 cup finely chopped scallions

Tofu: Cut the tofu into 16 cubes and set aside. In a medium bowl, combine the cornstarch, cornmeal, salt, white pepper, and red pepper flakes. Add the cubed tofu and coat well. Transfer the tofu to the air fryer basket. Spritz with the sesame oil. Cook for 20 minutes at 350°F, shaking gently halfway through the cooking time.

Peanut Sauce: Pulse the ginger, garlic, peanut butter, tamari, lime juice, maple syrup, and chili paste in a blender until smooth. Add water, if needed for a thick consistency that is thin enough to drizzle. To serve, transfer the tofu to a serving platter. Pour the peanut sauce into a small dipping bowl and top with the scallions.

Serves 4

No-Oil Option: Omit the sesame oil.

Breaded Mushrooms

Let's make simple fried mushrooms a bit more sophisticated, shall we? I use portobello mushrooms, because they are so meaty and easier to handle when breading and frying without a lot of oil.

> 2 large portobello mushroom caps, lightly rinsed and patted dry
> 1/2 cup soy flour
> 1/2 teaspoon granulated onion
> 1/4 teaspoon dried oregano
> 1/4 teaspoon dried basil
> 1/4 teaspoon granulated garlic
> 1/2 teaspoon black pepper, divided
> 1/2 cup ice cold water
> 2 tablespoons Follow Your Heart VeganEgg or 1 Flax Egg (page 16)
> 1/8 cup soymilk
> 1 teaspoon low-sodium tamari
> 1 cup panko bread crumbs
> 1/4 teaspoon sea salt
> 1 to 2 spritzes canola oil or extra-virgin olive oil

Cut the portobello caps into 1/4-inch thick slices. Combine the flour, granulated onion, oregano, basil, granulated garlic, and 1/4 teaspoon of the pepper in a shallow dish or plate.

Whisk together the water and VeganEgg. Pour the mixture into a shallow bowl. Add the soymilk and tamari. Pour the panko bread crumbs into a third shallow dish or plate and add the salt and remaining black pepper, mixing well.

Working in batches, place the mushrooms in the flour mixture, dredging to coat them well. Shake off any excess flour and dip the mushrooms in the milk mixture. Shake off any excess liquid, then place the mushrooms in the bread crumbs and coat them well. Place the breaded mushrooms on a plate covered with parchment paper and repeat this process until all the mushrooms are breaded.

Spray the air fryer basket with the oil. Place the breaded mushrooms in the air fryer basket (you may have to do this in batches) and cook at 360°F for 7 minutes, shaking halfway through the cooking time.

Serves 2 to 4

Note

To gill or not to gill? Many recipes call for scraping out the black "gills" after stemming the portobello cap. I say leave 'em there. Because we're cooking these quickly, we don't need to worry about the final product discoloring. Besides, it makes the fried mushrooms even meatier!

Vegan Wings

These chicken-friendly, plant-based wings are super compassionate and super spicy. Though using homemade seitan is always nice, I really love using packaged seitan for this recipe. In a matter of minutes, you can serve them over a vegan Caesar salad or roll the wings and lettuce up in a large whole wheat tortilla for a hearty sandwich wrap.

1/4 cup nondairy butter
1/2 cup Frank's RedHot Original Cayenne Pepper Sauce or your favorite cayenne hot sauce
2 cloves garlic
16 to 18 ounces Baked Chick'n-Style Seitan (page 124), cut into 8 to 10 pieces, or WestSoy or Pacific brands chicken-style seitan
1/4 cup chickpea flour
1/4 cup cornmeal

Combine the butter, hot sauce, and garlic in a small saucepan over medium heat for 3 to 5 minutes. Pour half of the sauce in a bowl. Set aside.

Add the seitan pieces to the sauce in the pan. Mix well to coat the seitan.

Combine the flour and cornmeal in a shallow bowl.

Preheat the air fryer to 370°F for 3 minutes. Dredge the seitan pieces in the flour mixture, coating them well. Place the seitan in the air fryer. Cook at 370°F for 7 minutes, shaking at 3 minutes.

Transfer the wings to the bowl with the reserved hot sauce. Toss and serve with nondairy blue cheese or ranch dressing.

Serves 4

Note

These wings are spicy. If you want to cut the heat, reduce the amount of hot sauce and replace it with an equal amount of vegetable broth.

Roasted Barbecue Chickpeas

These are great as a snack eaten like nuts or sprinkled over a salad as a crouton. Chickpeas are a great source of protein and fiber, so it's a little hard to feel guilty if you happen to eat the entire batch.

> 1 (15-ounce) can chickpeas, drained, rinsed, and patted dry
> 1 teaspoon peanut oil
> 1/2 teaspoon maple syrup
> 1 teaspoon paprika
> 1 teaspoon garlic powder
> 1/2 teaspoon black pepper
> 1/2 teaspoon ground mustard
> 1/2 teaspoon chipotle powder

Combine the chickpeas, oil, and maple syrup in a large bowl, tossing the chickpeas to coat. Sprinkle the paprika, garlic powder, pepper, mustard, and chipotle powder over the chickpeas and combine until all the chickpeas are well coated.

Transfer the chickpeas to the air fryer basket. Cook at 400°F for 15 minutes, shaking every 5 minutes.

Serves 4

No-Oil Option: Omit the peanut oil.

Note

Save that bean water when you drain the chickpeas! Known as aquafaba, the chickpea water can be used to make Onion Rings (page 80).

5

*O*ne of the things I enjoy most about my air fryer is the variety of ways it allows me to enjoy vegetables. If you follow a vegan diet, you know that we eat lots of vegetables, and we sometimes get into a habit of the same preparations. One way to keep vegetables exciting is to experiment with textures and flavor profiles. And we sure are doing that in this chapter! These recipes are great as sides with lunch or dinner.

On the Side

Balsamic Herbed Tomatoes

This is an aromatic tomato recipe that shows up regularly in our meal rotation as a colorful, nutritious side dish. Cook the tomatoes longer and you have quickie stewed tomatoes for sauces and soups. Note that firm, red tomatoes are ideal, as they stand up to the heat incredibly well.

1/4 cup balsamic vinegar
1/2 teaspoon coarse sea salt
1/4 teaspoon ground black pepper
1 tablespoon dried oregano
1 teaspoon red pepper flakes
2 large, firm tomatoes, each cut into 4 slices
Extra-virgin olive oil spray

Pour the vinegar into a shallow dish. Stir in the salt, pepper, oregano, and red pepper flakes.

Dip each tomato slice into the vinegar mixture. Preheat the air fryer to 360°F for 3 minutes.

Arrange the tomatoes, in a single layer, on a grill insert or directly in the air fryer (you should be able to cook 2 to 4 slices at a time, depending upon the size of your air fryer). To increase the cooking capacity, place a rack accessory over the grill insert or basket, which will allow for two layers of tomatoes to cook at once.

Spoon the remaining vinegar mixture over each tomato. Spritz the oil over the tomatoes. Cook at 360°F for 5 to 6 minutes. Remove the tomatoes carefully with a spatula.

Serves 4

No-Oil Option: Omit the olive oil spray.

NOTE

To make "stewed" tomatoes, cook at 400°F for 6 minutes. Add the tomatoes to a recipe using tomatoes (such as soup, chili, or marinara sauce) or store them in an airtight container to use later (you can store them up to 3 days in the refrigerator). They will fall apart from the roasting, and that's a good thing!

Parsnip Fries

As a vegan cooking coach, I swoop into a client's kitchen and work side by side with them to prepare a week's worth of food. I leave them with a set of skills by which they can continue plant-based cooking on their own. One client, Laura, loves parsnips. She and I jump-started this recipe. This sweet root vegetable tastes terrific here with the peppery spices.

2 medium parsnips, trimmed and well washed
1 teaspoon avocado oil or canola oil
1 teaspoon ground cinnamon
1/2 teaspoon ground cumin
1/2 teaspoon paprika
1/2 teaspoon ground coriander
1/2 teaspoon sea salt
1/4 teaspoon black pepper
1/2 teaspoon cornstarch
1 tablespoon spelt flour or brown rice flour

Trim the tops and bottoms of the parsnips. Slice in half lengthwise. Halve or quarter the thick parts lengthwise, until all parsnip pieces are roughly the same size.

Transfer them to a large bowl. Add the oil, cinnamon, cumin, paprika, coriander, salt, and pepper.

In a small bowl, combine the cornstarch and flour. Sprinkle the cornstarch mixture over the parsnips and toss with tongs until well coated.

Cook the parsnips at 370°F for 15 minutes, or until golden brown, shaking halfway through the cooking time.

Serves 2 to 4

No-Oil Option: Omit the avocado oil.

Buffalo Cauliflower

Hot and *spicy* are two culinary terms that we love in our kitchen. Jessica Schoech, a member of my Facebook group, Vegan Air Frying Enthusiasts, offered an online class demonstrating a flavorful air-fried Buffalo cauliflower that demystified using batter in the air fryer. Following is my take, with fewer steps, inspired by that class.

1 large head cauliflower
1 cup unbleached all-purpose flour
1 teaspoon vegan chicken bouillon granules (or Butler Chik-Style Seasoning)
1/4 teaspoon cayenne pepper
1/4 teaspoon chili powder
1/4 teaspoon paprika
1/4 teaspoon dried chipotle chile flakes
1 cup soymilk
Canola oil spray
2 tablespoons nondairy butter
1/2 cup Frank's RedHot Original Cayenne Pepper Sauce or your favorite cayenne hot sauce
2 cloves garlic, minced

Cut the cauliflower into bite-size pieces. Rinse and drain the cauliflower pieces.

Combine the flour, bouillon granules, cayenne, chili powder, paprika, and chipotle flakes in a large bowl. Slowly whisk in the milk until a thick batter is formed.

Spray the air fryer basket with canola oil and preheat the air fryer to 390°F for 10 minutes.

While the air fryer is preheating, toss the cauliflower in the batter. Transfer the battered cauliflower to the air fryer basket. Cook for 20 minutes on 390°F. Using tongs, turn the cauliflower pieces at 10 minutes (don't be alarmed if they stick).

After turning the cauliflower, heat the butter, hot sauce, and garlic in a small saucepan over medium-hight heat. Bring the mixture to a boil, reduce the heat to simmer, and cover. Once the cauliflower is cooked, transfer it to a large bowl. Pour the sauce over the cauliflower and toss gently with tongs. Serve immediately.

Serves 2 to 4

Note

This is one messy dish. The batter may drip through mesh air fryer baskets. Not to worry; air fryers are easy to clean!

On the Side

Cheesy Dill Polenta Bites

Add a little coconut milk and nutritional yeast when cooking polenta to achieve the elusive flavor and texture of dairy foods. Shelf-stable light culinary coconut milk can be found in cans or cartons in the ethnic aisle of the grocery store or with other shelf-stable plant-based milks. These bites are a tasty snack: dip them in marinara sauce or nondairy ranch dressing to up the flavor ante.

1 cup light culinary coconut milk
3 cups vegetable broth
3 cloves garlic, minced
1/2 teaspoon ground turmeric
1/2 teaspoon dried dill
1 cup dried polenta or cornmeal
1 tablespoon nondairy butter
2 tablespoons nutritional yeast
1 teaspoon fresh lemon juice
Canola oil spray

For the Polenta:

In a pressure cooker or Instant Pot: Combine the milk, broth, garlic, turmeric, dill, and polenta in an uncovered pressure cooker (or a multicooker, such as an Instant Pot). Cover the pressure cooker and bring to pressure. Cook on high pressure for 5 minutes. Use a natural release after 15 minutes. If using a multicooker, choose manual and high pressure for 5 minutes. Remove the lid and stir in the butter, nutritional yeast, and lemon juice.

On the stovetop: Bring the milk, broth, garlic, turmeric, and dill to a boil over medium-high heat in a large saucepan. Pour the polenta slowly into the boiling milk mixture, whisking constantly until all the polenta is incorporated and there are no lumps. Reduce the heat to low and simmer, whisking often, until the polenta starts to thicken, about 5 minutes. The polenta should still be slightly loose. Cover the saucepan and cook for 30 minutes, whisking every 5 to 6 minutes. When the polenta is too thick to whisk, stir it with a wooden spoon. The polenta is done when its texture is creamy and the individual grains are tender. Turn off the heat and gently stir the butter into the polenta until the butter partially melts. Mix the nutritional yeast and lemon juice into the polenta. Cover the saucepan and let the polenta stand 5 minutes to thicken.

Set the hot polenta aside to cool (you can transfer the polenta to a medium bowl and refrigerate for 15 minutes to speed up the process).

For the Polenta Bites:

Roll 1/8-cup scoops of polenta into balls and arrange them in the air fryer in a single layer. (Depending upon the size of your air fryer, you may have to cook in batches.) Spritz them with the canola oil. Cook at 400°F for 12 to 14 minutes, shaking at 6 minutes.

Makes 20 polenta bites

No-Oil Option: Omit the butter and oil spray.

Tip

Buy a tube of shelf-stable polenta. Slice and coat in nutritional yeast and dried dill. Cook at 400°F for 12 to 14 minutes, shaking at 6 minutes.

Roasted Brussels Sprouts

The first time I tried Brussels sprouts in the air fryer, I knew it was a game changer. The crispy brown leaves surrounding the tender insides were ready in twelve minutes instead of thirty, and that's all I needed to know. I'm a big fan of Asian-style savory sauces and marinades, as you'll see in this recipe.

1 pound Brussels sprouts
2 tablespoons soy sauce
1 tablespoon rice vinegar
1 teaspoon canola oil
1 tablespoon minced garlic
1/2 teaspoon white pepper

Trim the bottoms of the Brussels sprouts, and slice each sprout in half from top to bottom (the outer leaves will fall off easily). Rinse and drain. Transfer the Brussels sprouts to a large bowl.

Whisk together the soy sauce, vinegar, oil, garlic, and white pepper in a small bowl. Pour over the Brussels sprouts. Toss gently with tongs, coating well.

Preheat the air fryer to 390°F for 3 minutes. Transfer the Brussels sprouts to the air fryer basket. Cook for 12 minutes, shaking halfway through the cooking time.

Serves 4 to 6

No-Oil Option: Omit the canola oil.

Roasted Acorn Squash

This is simple to prepare and my no-oil approach to garlic butter (or, in this case, sauce) makes it an all-around wholesome dish. You have a couple of fun serving options, too. Simply slice and serve the squash halves as sides or use each half as an edible serving vessel for things like brown rice or quinoa. For a beautiful sweet and savory appetizer, fill each half with the Caramelized Fruit-and-Nut Topping (page 167) or the caramelized pear and onion used in the Gourmet Grilled Cheese (page 137).

1 (16-ounce) acorn squash, washed
1/4 cup vegetable broth
2 tablespoons nutritional yeast
3 cloves garlic, minced

Split the squash in half and scoop out the seeds with a spoon. (Set the seeds aside to make the Tamari Squash Seeds on page 79). Slice off the end of each piece to make a flat bottom.

Place each squash half in the air fryer, flesh-side up. Cook at 360°F for 10 minutes.

In a small bowl, whisk together the broth, nutritional yeast, and garlic.

After 10 minutes, open the air fryer basket and pour 1/8 cup of the garlic sauce over one squash half and 1/8 cup over the other squash half. The sauce will settle into the "bowl" of the squash. Use a brush to coat the top of the squash. Increase the heat to 390°F and continue cooking for 5 minutes longer, until the squash is tender.

Remove the squash halves from the air fryer and slice them or use them as edible serving bowls.

Serves 2

Tamari Squash Seeds

Sure, pumpkin seeds are all the rage, but let's not waste the delectable seeds found in the butternut and acorn squash. They are a great source of fiber and they pack a protein punch.

> 1/4 to 1/2 cup acorn or butternut squash seeds (the amount varies by the size of squash)
>
> 2 tablespoons low-sodium tamari or low-sodium soy sauce
>
> 1/4 teaspoon white pepper or freshly ground black pepper

Rinse the squash seeds well, removing any strings or bits of squash. Transfer them to a small bowl or measuring cup. Pour the tamari over the seeds and let them marinate for 30 minutes.

Drain (but don't rinse) the seeds.

Preheat the air fryer to 390°F for 3 minutes. Transfer the seeds to the air fryer basket and sprinkle with the white pepper. Cook at 390°F for 6 minutes, shaking halfway through the cooking time. Eat the seeds immediately or store them in an airtight container for 3 days.

Serves 1 to 2

Onion Rings

Vegans miss onion rings! Commonly made with eggs and buttermilk, vegan versions are rarely available at restaurants or in the frozen food aisle of a grocery store. (But if you find Alexia or Ian's brands onion rings at the store, grab 'em: they're vegan!). In this recipe, aquafaba (canned-chickpea water) stands in for the egg.

1 large onion, cut into 1/4-inch thick slices
1 cup unbleached all-purpose flour
1/4 cup chickpea flour
1 teaspoon baking powder
1 teaspoon sea salt
1/2 cup aquafaba or vegan egg substitute (see page 16)
1 cup soymilk
3/4 cup panko bread crumbs

Preheat the air fryer to 360°F for 5 minutes. Separate the onion slices into rings.

Combine the all-purpose flour, chickpea flour, baking powder, and salt in a small bowl.

Dredge the onion slices in the flour mixture until well coated. Set aside.

Whisk the aquafaba and milk into the remaining flour mixture. Dip the floured onion rings into the batter to coat.

Spread the panko bread crumbs on a plate or shallow dish and dredge the rings into the crumbs, covering well.

Place the onion rings into the air fryer in a single layer and cook for 7 minutes at 360°F, shaking halfway through the cooking time. If you have a smaller air fryer, you may have to cook in batches.

Serves 2 to 4

Maple Butternut Squash

This is one of my favorite winter squash varieties. Not only is it a warm, comforting fall food, but it's high in fiber and potassium. Great-tasting food that's good for you is a win-win. Serve this roasted vegetable as a side with baked tofu and steamed vegetables or tossed with sautéed greens. Save those seeds to make Tamari Squash Seeds (page 79).

1 large butternut squash, peeled, halved, seeded, and cut into 1-inch chunks
1 teaspoon extra-virgin olive oil or canola oil
2 tablespoons maple syrup
1 teaspoon ground cinnamon
1/2 teaspoon ground cardamom
1/2 teaspoon dried thyme
1/2 teaspoon sea salt

Preheat the air fryer to 390°F. Place the squash into a large mixing bowl. Add the oil, maple syrup, cinnamon, cardamom, thyme, and salt and toss to coat the squash.

Transfer the squash to the air fryer basket. Cook for 20 minutes or until browned, shaking halfway through the cooking time.

Serves 4

No-Oil Option: Omit the olive oil.

Kale Chips

Crunchy, leafy green chips are becoming easy to find in grocery stores, but the price tag on kale chips is rather surprising. Though kale chips are traditionally dehydrated or baked at low temperatures—common in raw vegan cooking—this is an easy way to make crispy kale chips fast. A word of caution: some air fryers really blow the pieces of kale around. While some accessories include a cover, which keeps the kale away from the heating element, if you pay heed to the kale-massage step in the recipes, the added weight of the oil helps keep the kale in the basket.

8 cups stemmed kale
1 teaspoon canola oil or extra-virgin olive oil
1 teaspoon rice vinegar
1 teaspoon soy sauce
2 tablespoons nutritional yeast

Wash and drain the kale. Transfer it to a large bowl. Tear the kale into 2-inch pieces. Avoid tearing pieces too small, as some air fryers, with powerful forced air, may pull the kale into the heating element.

Add the oil, vinegar, soy sauce, and nutritional yeast to the bowl. Using your hands, massage all the ingredients into the kale for about 2 minutes.

Transfer the kale to the air fryer basket. Cook at 360°F for 5 minutes. Shake the basket. Increase the heat to 390°F and cook for 5 to 7 more minutes.

Serves 2 to 4

No-Oil Option: Omit the canola oil.

Note

Don't be concerned if you eat the whole batch. It's kale. You're fine.

Fried Green Tomatoes

I love fried green tomatoes, though I seldom made them. Notice I used the past tense. Now, I make them often, because air-frying is so easy and the texture is fantastic. They're great as an appetizer or side dish, and I also love them tossed in a salad.

1/2 cup potato starch
1 cup soy flour, divided
1/4 cup soymilk
2 tablespoons nutritional yeast
1/2 to 1 teaspoon hot sauce
1/4 cup almond flour
1/4 cup panko bread crumbs
1 teaspoon smoked paprika
1 teaspoon sea salt
1/4 teaspoon black pepper
2 large green or heirloom tomatoes, cut into 1/2-inch thick slices
2 to 4 spritzes canola oil

In a shallow dish, combine the potato starch and 1/2 cup of the soy flour.

In a second shallow dish, combine the milk, nutritional yeast, and hot sauce.

In a third shallow dish, combine the remaining 1/2 cup soy flour, almond flour, panko bread crumbs, smoked paprika, salt, and pepper.

Coat the tomatoes in the potato starch mixture. Shake off any excess starch and then dip the tomatoes in the milk mixture to coat. Shake off any excess milk and then dredge the tomatoes in the seasoned soy flour mixture.

Spritz the air fryer basket with the oil. Place as many tomatoes on the air fryer basket as you can. Spritz the top of the tomatoes with more oil.

Cook at 320°F for 3 minutes. Shake the air fryer basket gently. Increase the heat to 400°F and cook for 2 more minutes.

Makes 6 to 8 fried green tomatoes

No-Oil Option: Omit the canola oil.

Eggplant Parmesan

There's only one way you can get me to eat eggplant, and that's breaded and fried. You likely have all the ingredients on hand, and while the eggplant is cooking in the air fryer, you can heat up your favorite marinara sauce on the stove. It's a fast meal that looks rather fancy.

1 medium eggplant
1/2 cup unbleached all-purpose flour
1 Flax Egg (page 16) or equivalent Follow Your Heart VeganEgg or Ener-G Egg Replacer
1 1/2 cups panko bread crumbs
2 to 4 spritzes extra-virgin olive oil
1/2 cup marinara sauce
1/2 cup shredded nondairy Parmesan cheese

Wash the eggplant and pat dry. Slice the eggplant, making 8 (1/2-inch thick) rounds.

Set up a three-part dredging station using three shallow bowls, with the flour in the first, flax egg in the second, and panko bread crumbs in the third. Spritz the air fryer basket with the oil.

Dredge an eggplant round into the flour, coating well. Dip the eggplant round into the flax egg, and then dredge it in the panko bread crumbs. Shake off any excess bread crumbs and place the eggplant round into the air fryer basket. Repeat this process with more of the eggplant rounds. If you have a rack accessory, place it in the air fryer basket and continue coating the remaining eggplant rounds and place them on the rack. If you have a smaller air fryer or no rack to add a second level of cooking, air-fry the eggplant rounds in 2 or 3 batches. Spritz the top of each eggplant round with olive oil. Cook at 360°F for 12 minutes, until golden brown.

Heat the marinara sauce in a small saucepan over medium heat.

After 12 minutes, open the air fryer and add 1 tablespoon cheese to each eggplant round and cook for 2 minutes longer. To serve, plate 2 eggplant rounds per person on a small plate. Spoon 2 tablespoons marinara sauce over the eggplant.

Serves 4

No-Oil Option: Omit the olive oil.

Mixed Vegetable Fritters

This is a fun alternative to a vegan burger. Full of veggies, these little gems also boast nutrient-boosting flaxseed and peas.

3 tablespoons ground flaxseed
1/2 cup water
2 medium russet potatoes
2 cups frozen mixed vegetables (carrots, peas, and corn), thawed and drained
1 cup frozen peas, thawed and drained
1/2 cup coarsely chopped onion
1/4 cup finely chopped fresh cilantro
1/2 cup unbleached all-purpose flour
1/2 teaspoon sea salt
Extra-virgin olive oil for spritzing

In a small bowl, make a flax egg by mixing the flaxseed and water with a fork or small whisk.

Peel the potatoes and shred them into a bowl. (Or use the grater blade in a food processor; if doing so, transfer the shredded potatoes back into a bowl.) Add the mixed vegetables and onion to the potatoes. Add the cilantro and flax egg and stir to combine. Add the flour and salt and combine well. Preheat the air fryer to 360°F for 3 minutes.

Scoop out 1/3 cup of the potato mixture to form a patty. Repeat this process until all of the mixture is used to make fritter patties.

Spritz the fritters with the oil. Transfer the fritters to the air fryer basket (you may need to do several batches, depending upon the size of your air fryer). Cook the fritters for 15 minutes, flipping halfway through the cooking time.

Makes 10 to 12 fritters

No-Oil Option: Omit the olive oil.

Potatoes Are the Air Fryer's BFF

And now, a nod to the spud. Because, as much as I'm delighted by the fact that you can make so many other things in an air fryer, potatoes truly do cook up beautifully. Potatoes have gotten a bad rap in this low-carb nation, but let us not forget that good carbs are, well, good. Eat your potatoes!

Cheesy Potato Wedges

I grew up in the Midwest where potato skins were a staple in most restaurants. These days, I'm still a fan of the potato skin, but I want that potato, too. This is a fun recipe to make for game-day noshing.

Potatoes
1 pound fingerling potatoes
1 teaspoon extra-virgin olive oil
1 teaspoon kosher salt
1 teaspoon ground black pepper
1/2 teaspoon garlic powder

Cheese Sauce
1/2 cup raw cashews
1/2 teaspoon ground turmeric
1/2 teaspoon paprika
2 tablespoons nutritional yeast
1 teaspoon fresh lemon juice
2 tablespoons to 1/4 cup water

Potatoes: Preheat the air fryer to 400°F for 3 minutes. Wash the potatoes. Cut the potatoes in half lengthwise and transfer them to a large bowl. Add the oil, salt, pepper, and garlic powder to the potatoes. Toss to coat. Transfer the potatoes to the air fryer. Cook for 16 minutes, shaking halfway through the cooking time.

Cheese Sauce: Combine the cashews, turmeric, paprika, nutritional yeast, and lemon juice in a high-speed blender. Blend on low, slowly increasing the speed and adding water as needed. Be careful to avoid using too much water, as you want a thick, cheesy consistency.

Transfer the cooked potatoes to an air fryer–safe pan or a piece of parchment paper. Drizzle the cheese sauce over the potato wedges. Place the pan in the air fryer and cook for 2 more minutes at 400°F.

Serves 4

No-Oil Option: Omit the olive oil.

Hasselback Potatoes

This twist on a traditional baked potato changes the texture: think crispy, like chips. Spoon chili or split pea soup over it and you've got yourself a meal.

2 medium russet potatoes
2 spritzes extra-virgin olive oil
1/4 teaspoon sea salt
2 pinches black pepper
1 teaspoon minced garlic

Wash the potatoes well. To cut the potatoes, lay them down on their flattest sides in a large spoon (to prevent you from slicing all the way through them). With a sharp knife, slice down from the top until the knife makes contact with the spoon. Make 1/8-inch slices across the potatoes.

Spritz the potatoes with the oil (or brush them with vegetable broth) and sprinkle half of the salt and a pinch black pepper on each. Place the potatoes in the air fryer and cook for 20 minutes at 390°F.

Remove the basket from the air fryer and press 1/2 teaspoon garlic in between the slices of each potato. Return the potatoes to the air fryer and cook for another 15 to 20 minutes. (The total cooking time should be about 35 to 40 minutes; longer if using large potatoes.)

Serves 2

No-Oil Option: Use vegetable broth instead of olive oil.

Poutine

Poutine (pronounced "poo-tin") is a Canadian dish—originating in Quebec—that is pretty simple: French fries, gravy, and cheese curds. Here's a vegan version that could be a meal if you use my Mushroom White Bean Gravy (page 94).

> 3 medium russet potatoes, cut into 1/4-inch slices, and cut again into 1/4-inch strips
> 1 teaspoon peanut oil or canola oil
> 2 cups Mushroom White Bean Gravy (page 94) or Pacific or Imagine brands mushroom gravy
> 1/2 cup coarsely chopped Daiya Jalapeño Havarti Style Farmhouse Block cheese or Follow Your Heart shredded Parmesan cheese

Rinse the potato fries in cold water. Soak for 20 minutes. Rinse, drain, and pat the potatoes dry with a paper towel. Transfer the fries to a large bowl and toss with the peanut oil.

Place the fries in the air fryer basket and cook for 20 minutes at 390°F, shaking halfway through the cooking time.

While the fries are cooking, make the gravy.

When the fries are fully cooked, place them on 4 serving dishes. Sprinkle 2 tablespoons cheese and then spoon 1/2 cup gravy over each serving.

Serves 4

No-Oil Option: Omit the peanut oil.

Mushroom White Bean Gravy

1/4 cup nondairy butter
3 cloves garlic, coarsely chopped
1/2 cup coarsely chopped yellow onion
1 cup coarsely chopped shiitake mushrooms
1/8 teaspoon dried sage
1/8 teaspoon dried rosemary
1/8 teaspoon ground black pepper
1 1/4 cups vegetable broth
1/4 cup low-sodium soy sauce
1 (15-ounce) can white beans, drained and rinsed
1/8 to 1/4 cup nutritional yeast flakes

Heat the butter in a small saucepan over medium-high heat. Add the garlic and onion and sauté until the onion is translucent. Add the mushrooms, sage, rosemary, and pepper. Mix well. Stir in the broth and soy sauce. Bring the mixture to a boil.

Add the beans. Use an immersion blender in the saucepan to blend the gravy for 20 to 30 seconds, or until smooth. Alternatively, you can transfer the gravy to a blender and blend until smooth, then return the gravy back to the saucepan after blending.

Cover the saucepan, reduce the heat to medium, and cook for 5 minutes, stirring occasionally. Add the nutritional yeast, stir well, then cover the saucepan and simmer for 5 minutes longer, stirring as needed.

Makes about 2 1/2 cups

Sweet Potato Fries

This recipe is a nod to a now closed restaurant in Jim Thorpe, Pennsylvania. The fries at FLOW were so good that I begged the chef to share his secret: beer. Here's my take.

2 large white sweet potatoes, cut into 1/4-inch slices, and cut again into 1/4-inch strips
1/4 cup dark vegan beer
1 teaspoon red miso
1 teaspoon canola oil
1 tablespoon light brown sugar
1 teaspoon ground cinnamon
1/2 teaspoon ground cumin
1/2 teaspoon sea salt

Rinse the fries in cold water. Transfer the fries to a large bowl. In a small bowl, whisk together the beer, miso, and oil. Drizzle the beer mixture over the fries, toss well, and set aside for 20 minutes.

Drain the fries and return them to the bowl. Sprinkle the brown sugar, cinnamon, cumin, and salt over the fries. Toss until well coated. Cook the fries for 15 to 20 minutes at 320°F, until golden brown.

Serves 2 to 3

No-Oil Option: Omit the canola oil.

Kale and Potato Nuggets

These bites may seem naughty but they are really nutritious and, most importantly, tasty! This is a great way to use leftover mashed potatoes—just skip the part about cooking the potatoes. and use leftover mashers instead.

    2 cups finely chopped potatoes
    1 teaspoon extra-virgin olive oil or canola oil
    1 clove garlic, minced
    4 cups loosely packed coarsely chopped kale
    1/8 cup almond milk
    1/4 teaspoon sea salt
    1/8 teaspoon ground black pepper
    Vegetable oil spray, as needed

Add the potatoes to a large saucepan of boiling water. Cook until tender, about 30 minutes.

In a large skillet, heat the oil over medium-high heat. Add the garlic and sauté until golden brown. Add the kale and sauté for 2 to 3 minutes. Transfer to a large bowl.

Drain the cooked potatoes and transfer them to a medium bowl. Add the milk, salt, and pepper and mash with a fork or potato masher. Transfer the potatoes to the large bowl and combine with the cooked kale.

Preheat the air fryer to 390°F for 5 minutes.

Roll the potato and kale mixture into 1-inch nuggets. Spritz the air fryer basket with vegetable oil. Place the nuggets in the air fryer and cook for 12 to 15 minutes, until golden brown, shaking at 6 minutes.

Serves 4

No-Oil Option: Omit the olive oil.

Umami Fries

As mentioned in chapter 2, some believe umami—considered the fifth taste in Japanese culinary cuisine—is the secret ingredient to vegan cooking. It adds a meaty, savory flavor and the Marmite and cider do just that to these fries.

> 2 large russet potatoes, scrubbed
> 1/4 cup hot water
> 1 tablespoon Marmite or Vegemite
> 1 tablespoon apple cider vinegar

Cut the potatoes into 1/4-inch slices, then cut the slices into 1/4-inch strips.

Transfer the fries to a shallow baking pan or rimmed baking sheet.

Pour the water into a blender. Turn the blender on low and slowly drizzle in the Marmite. Add the vinegar, increase the blender's speed to high, and blend for just a few seconds. Pour the Marmite mixture over the fries. Toss the fries with tongs or use your hands to make sure the fries are coated with marinade. Cover and set aside for about 15 minutes.

Preheat the air fryer to 360°F for 3 minutes. Drain the fries and transfer them to the air fryer. Cook at 360°F for 16 to 20 minutes, shaking halfway through the cooking time.

Serves 2 to 4

When my coaching clients ask me how they will get enough protein, I know that the real question is, "How do I replace the meat on my plate?" Plant foods, especially legumes and beans, can make hearty, protein-rich entrees, and you'll find them in almost all of these main dish recipes. This chapter features a balance of whole foods, such as Baked Gigante Beans (page 112), with vegan versions of some old favorites such as pot pie, meatballs, and even corn dogs.

Main Dishes

Let's Talk Tofu

These three simple tofu techniques deliver consistently good results.

- **Freeze First.** To give tofu a chewy texture, freeze your water-packed tofu before using it. Just toss it in the freezer, still in the package, until you're ready to use it. Before you plan to cook with it, thaw it overnight in the refrigerator. Drain and press the tofu (page 13) and transfer it to an airtight container. I prefer a rectangle container, just a bit larger than the block of tofu (such as the TofuXpress pressing device).

- **Marvelous Marinades.** Marinades almost always include a liquid (vegetable oil or vegetable broth), an acid (any kind of vinegar, tomato sauce, or fresh lemon, lime, or orange juice), and a variety of spices (choose spices that match the flavor profile for the meal: Indian, Mexican, Italian, Moroccan, and so on).

- **Patience Pays Off.** Pour that marinade over the pressed tofu, cover the container, and place it in the refrigerator ideally for at least 1 hour (although 8 hours is ideal).

Basic Air-Fried Tofu

Putting theory to practice, try the tofu preparation explained in the sidebar on the facing page for all of your air-fried tofu, including this basic recipe.

1 (14-ounce) package extra-firm tofu, frozen, thawed, drained, and pressed (page 13)
1 teaspoon sesame oil
1/4 cup low-sodium soy sauce or tamari
2 tablespoons rice vinegar
2 teaspoons ground ginger, divided
2 teaspoons cornstarch or potato starch
1 teaspoon chickpea flour or brown rice flour

Cut the block of tofu into 12 cubes and transfer them to an airtight container.

In a small bowl, whisk together the oil, soy sauce, vinegar, and 1 teaspoon of the ginger. Pour the oil mixture over the cubed tofu, cover the container, and place in the refrigerator to marinate for at least 1 hour (ideally 8 hours).

Drain the marinated tofu and transfer it to a medium bowl. In a small bowl, combine the cornstarch, chickpea flour, and the remaining 1 teaspoon ginger. Sprinkle the cornstarch mixture over the drained tofu and gently toss with tongs, coating all the pieces of tofu.

Transfer the tofu to the air fryer. Cook at 350°F for 20 minutes. Shake at 10 minutes.

Serves 4

No-Oil Option: Omit the sesame oil.

Mongolian Tofu

I often say the sole reason that I bought an air fryer was for tofu. If you, too, struggle to achieve just the right texture, this recipe will make you a believer in the power of the air fryer. The result is a crispy exterior and meaty interior, and it's divine served simply over brown rice or udon noodles.

Basic Air-Fried Tofu (page 103)
1/4 cup low-sodium soy sauce
1/4 cup water
1/8 cup sugar
3 cloves garlic, minced
1/4 teaspoon ground ginger

While the tofu is cooking in the air fryer, combine the soy sauce, water, sugar, garlic, and ginger in a saucepan over medium-high heat. Bring the mixture to a gentle boil, then immediately reduce the heat to low and simmer, stirring occasionally.

When the tofu is done, transfer it to the saucepan, gently folding the tofu into the sauce until all the cubes are coated. Cover and simmer on low for about 5 minutes (or until the tofu has absorbed the sauce).

Serves 4

Sesame-Crusted Tofu

I've always had trouble getting sesame seeds to adhere to tofu. Using a little potato starch with the sesame seeds is the first step to success. And, because the air fryer does all the cooking, don't flip that tofu!

- 1 (14-ounce) package extra-firm tofu, frozen, thawed, drained, and pressed (page 13)
- 1/4 cup tamari or soy sauce
- 1/8 cup rice vinegar
- 1/8 cup mirin (see note)
- 2 teaspoons sesame oil
- 2 teaspoons light or dark agave syrup or vegan honey
- 2 teaspoons minced garlic
- 1 teaspoon grated fresh ginger
- 1 to 2 spritzes canola oil
- 2 tablespoons black sesame seeds
- 2 tablespoons white sesame seeds
- 1 teaspoon potato starch

Place the tofu in an airtight container that is about the size of the block of tofu so that the marinade completely covers it. In a small bowl, combine the tamari, vinegar, mirin, sesame oil, agave, garlic, and ginger. Pour the marinade over the tofu, cover the container, and refrigerate for 1 to 8 hours (the longer the better).

Remove the tofu from the container and cut it in half lengthwise. Then cut each half in half lengthwise to form 4 tofu steaks. Rub both sides of each piece in the marinade.

Spritz the air fryer basket with the canola oil. Preheat the air fryer to 390°F for 3 minutes.

Sprinkle the black sesame seeds, white sesame seeds, and potato starch on a large plate. Combine well. Press a tofu steak into the seeds, flip over, and press the other side of the tofu into the seeds. Place the tofu in the air fryer basket and gently pat the seeds on top of the tofu into place. Add more seeds, if necessary, gently patting them into the tofu. Set the tofu slice aside on the plate.

Spritz the top of the tofu with additional canola oil. Cook at 390°F for 15 minutes. After about 7 minutes, gently use tongs to check that the tofu isn't sticking. (Do not flip the tofu!)

Serves 4

No-Oil Option: Replace the sesame oil in the marinade with vegetable broth. Omit the canola oil spritzes, but know that some of the sesame seeds may fly off the tofu while cooking and the texture may not be as crisp.

Note

Mirin is a sweet rice wine available in well-stocked supermarkets and Asian markets. If it's unavailable, increase the rice vinegar to 1/4 cup.

Main Dishes

Sambal Goreng Tempeh

A few years ago, I hosted an event all about tempeh with Seth Tibbott, founder of Tofurky. Seth was insistent that we include sambal goreng tempeh, a traditional Indonesian food that's fried, tossed in a hot sauce, and eaten by hand. My version requires a fork and is delicious served over white or sushi rice.

8 ounces tempeh, cut into 12 equal cubes
2 cups warm water
2 teaspoons sea salt
1/2 teaspoon ground turmeric
1 teaspoon canola oil or avocado oil
2 teaspoons Tofuna Fysh Sauce (page 11) or 1 teaspoon low-sodium soy sauce
    mixed with 1/4 teaspoon dulse flakes
4 cloves garlic
1/2 cup finely chopped onion
1 teaspoon chili garlic paste
1 teaspoon tamarind paste
2 tablespoons tomato paste
2 tablespoons water
2 teaspoons ponzu sauce

Place the tempeh in a medium bowl. In a medium measuring cup, mix together the warm water and salt and pour over the tempeh. Let the tempeh soak for 5 to 10 minutes.

Drain the tempeh and return it to the bowl. Add the turmeric, oil, and Tofuna Fysh Sauce, tossing with tongs to coat well.

Transfer the tempeh cubes to the air fryer basket. Cook at 320°F for 10 minutes. Shake the air fryer basket, increase the heat to 400°F, and cook for 5 minutes longer.

While the tempeh is in the air fryer, combine the garlic, onion, chili garlic paste, tamarind paste, tomato paste, water, and ponzu sauce in a food processor and pulse for 20 to 30 seconds. Transfer this mixture to a medium saucepan and bring it to a rapid boil on medium-high heat. Cover the sauce, reduce the heat to low, and simmer for 10 minutes.

Transfer the cooked tempeh to the saucepan and toss it in the sauce with a spoon or tongs to coat each piece well. Cover and simmer on low for 5 minutes.

Serves 4

Tempeh Kabobs

If you have the rack and skewer air fryer accessories, this is a different and fun way to serve up tempeh and veggies. You can also skewer the tempeh and vegetables and place them directly on the grill pan accessory or in the air fryer basket. These are terrific served over couscous.

8 ounces tempeh
3/4 cup low-sodium vegetable broth
Juice of 2 lemons
1/4 cup low-sodium tamari or soy sauce
2 teaspoons extra-virgin olive oil
1 teaspoon maple syrup or dark agave syrup
2 teaspoons ground cumin
1 teaspoon ground turmeric
1/2 teaspoon ground black pepper
3 cloves garlic, minced
1 medium red onion, quartered
1 small green bell pepper, thinly sliced
1 cup sliced, stemmed button mushrooms
1 cup halved cherry tomatoes

Steam the tempeh for 10 minutes in a saucepan on the stove. Alternatively, steam the tempeh for 1 minute on low pressure in an Instant Pot or pressure cooker; use a quick release. Combine the broth, lemon juice, tamari, oil, maple syrup, cumin, turmeric, pepper, and garlic in a medium bowl. Set aside.

Cut the tempeh into 12 cubes. Transfer them to an airtight container. Place the vegetables in a second airtight container. Pour half of the marinade over the tempeh and half over the vegetables. Cover both and refrigerate for 2 hours (or up to overnight). Drain the tempeh and vegetables, reserving the marinade.

Thread 3 cubes of tempeh, alternating each with the vegetables, on a skewer to make a kabob. Repeat this process to make 3 more kabobs. Place the kabobs in the air fryer basket or on the rack accessory. (If you are using a smaller air fryer, you may have to cook in two batches.) Cook at 390°F for 5 minutes. Turn the kabobs and drizzle remaining marinade over them. Cook for 5 more minutes.

Serves 4

No-Oil Option: Omit the olive oil.

Baked Gigante Beans

I love Greek food. It's a cuisine that allows simple vegetables and spices to sing. Gigante beans can almost always be found on the menu at a Greek restaurant, but they are not so easily found in a local grocery store. So, in this recipe, I call for butter beans. These are delicious served with Eggplant Parmesan (page 85).

1 1/2 cups cooked or canned butter beans or great Northern beans, rinsed and drained
1 teaspoon extra-virgin olive oil or canola oil
1 small onion, cut into 1/8-inch thick half-moon slices
1 clove garlic, minced
1 (8-ounce) can tomato sauce
1 tablespoon coarsely chopped fresh parsley
1/2 teaspoon dried oregano
1/2 teaspoon vegan chicken bouillon granules or salt (optional)
1/4 teaspoon freshly ground black pepper

Place the beans in an air fryer–safe casserole dish or pan.

Heat the oil in a medium saucepan on medium-high heat. Add the onion and garlic and sauté for 5 minutes. Add the tomato sauce, parsley, oregano, and bouillon granules. Bring the mixture to a boil, cover the saucepan, reduce the heat to low, and simmer for 3 minutes.

Preheat the air fryer to 360°F for 3 minutes. Pour the tomato mixture over the beans and mix well. Sprinkle the pepper over the beans. Place the beans in the air fryer basket. Cook at 360°F for 8 minutes.

Serves 2

No-Oil Option: Sauté the garlic and onion in vegetable broth or water instead of olive oil.

Personal Pizzas

I often use the air fryer as an oven. There's no need to waste the time and energy of preheating and then baking in a large oven when you're making small recipes. And the rapid-air heat makes a crispy pizza crust that cannot be beat.

4 ounces prepared Pizza Dough (page 14) or store-bought vegan pizza dough
2 spritzes extra-virgin olive oil
1/3 cup pizza sauce
1/3 cup nondairy shredded mozzarella cheese, divided
1/2 onion, cut into 1/8-inch thick half-moon slices
1/4 cup sliced mushrooms
2 to 3 black or green olives, pitted and sliced
4 fresh basil leaves

Place the pizza dough on a lightly floured work surface and roll it out or use your hands to press it out (keeping in mind the size of your air fryer basket, to assure it fits). Spritz the dough with the oil and place the dough, oiled side down, into the air fryer basket. Cook at 390°F for 4 to 5 minutes.

Once the dough is precooked, open the air fryer—use caution, as the basket is hot—and spread the sauce over the dough. Sprinkle half the cheese over the sauce. Add the onion, mushrooms, olives, and basil. Sprinkle the remaining cheese over the toppings.

Cook at 390°F for 6 minutes (or 7 to 8 minutes for a very crisp crust). Use a spatula to remove the pizza from the air fryer.

Serves 1

No-Oil Option: Omit the olive oil.

Fried Hot Dogs

Walter's Hot Dog Stand is a community treasure in my former hometown of Mamaroneck, New York. On weekends, a line formed down the block. What was so special about those hot dogs? They were split and grilled in butter. Here's a speedy, compassionate version. Serve with your favorite hot dog condiments. (Mine? Traditional ketchup, mustard, sweet relish, and raw onion!) You can step it up a notch by serving these with the Pretzel Hot Dog Buns (page 58).

    4 vegan hot dogs
    2 teaspoons nondairy butter
    4 Pretzel Hot Dog Buns (page 58) or store-bought vegan hot dog buns

Slice the hot dogs lengthwise without cutting all the way through them. Spread the hot dogs out flat, cut-side up. Spread 1/2 teaspoon butter on each hot dog.

Place the hot dogs, buttered side down, in the air fryer. Cook at 390°F for 3 minutes. Remove and set aside.

Place the hot dog buns in the air fryer and heat at 400°F for 1 minute to lightly toast them. Serve the hot dogs in the buns with your favorite condiments.

Serves 4

No-Oil Option: Omit the butter.

Corn Dogs

Hold on to your hat! You are about to make no-oil vegan corn dogs! This is a make-ahead recipe because the battered corn dog will need to sit in the freezer for a minimum of 2 hours before cooking for best results. You'll need wooden pointed corn dog sticks (5 1/2 x 3/16 inches) or skewers that will fit in the air fryer. Serve these with mustard and a side of Seasoned French Fries (page 44) for the consummate "anything you can eat, I can eat vegan" meal.

>   1/2 cup cornmeal
>   1/2 cup unbleached all-purpose flour
>   2 tablespoons granulated sugar
>   1 teaspoon baking powder
>   1/2 teaspoon paprika
>   1/2 teaspoon ground mustard
>   1/4 teaspoon salt
>   1/8 teaspoon black pepper
>   1/2 cup ice cold water
>   2 tablespoons Follow Your Heart VeganEgg
>   1/2 cup soymilk
>   6 vegan hot dogs

In a large bowl, combine the cornmeal, flour, sugar, baking powder, paprika, mustard, salt, and pepper.

In a small bowl, whisk together the water and VeganEgg. Add the milk and combine well. Slowly fold the water mixture into the cornmeal mixture, whisking to create a smooth batter. Pour the batter into a tall mason jar or drinking glass. Preheat the air fryer to 390°F for 5 minutes.

Lay out 6 (3 x 5-inch) pieces of parchment paper (big enough to roll each battered corn dog). Place 1 hot dog on a wooden stick and dip it into the batter. Place the corn dog on a parchment paper square and roll up the battered hot dog. Repeat this process with the remaining hot dogs. The last one may get messy; if necessary, place it in on a plate, and scrape the remaining batter out of the mason jar, and rub the batter onto the hot dog before rolling it up in parchment paper.

Place the wrapped corn dogs in a large freezer bag, laying it out flat in the freezer. Chill in the freezer for a minimum of 2 hours.

Remove the battered corn dogs from the freezer and unwrap them. Place a piece of parchment paper on the air fryer basket (enough to cover the bottom but with no excess paper above the bottom of the basket). Place the corn dogs on the parchment paper. You may have to do this in batches depending upon the size of the air fryer; if so, leave any remaining corn dogs in the freezer until you're ready to use them. Cook at 390°F for 12 minutes.

Serves 6

Stuffed Baked Potatoes

This is a great way to make leftovers exciting. Air-fry a wholesome baked potato and top it with leftover stew or chili. This is comfort food at its easiest!

2 medium russet potatoes, scrubbed
1 cup leftover homemade chili or stew or 1 (15-ounce) can vegan chili or stew
1/2 cup nondairy shredded cheddar or mozzarella cheese
1/4 cup nondairy sour cream
2 tablespoons finely chopped chives

Pierce the potatoes with a fork and arrange them in the air fryer basket. Cook at 390°F for 30 minutes.

Heat the chili on the stovetop or in the microwave until it is hot.

Carefully remove the potatoes from the basket and slice them lengthwise without cutting all the way through. Spoon 1/2 cup of the hot chili into each potato. Add 1/4 cup cheese over each potato.

Return the potatoes to the air fryer and continue cooking at 390°F for 5 to 10 minutes longer. Serve the potatoes with a dollop of sour cream and chives.

Serves 2

Fried Green Beans and Bacon

A traditional dish from the South, the haricots verts are the star in this dish while the vegan bacon takes a supporting role.

> 6 ounces Tempeh Bacon (page 30) or store-bought vegan bacon
> 1 teaspoon Vegan Magic or DIY "Vegan Magic" (page 17)
> 1 teaspoon granulated sugar
> 12 ounces fresh haricots verts (French green beans)

Place the bacon in the air fryer basket. Cook at 390°F for 5 minutes.

In an air fryer–safe pan, combine the Vegan Magic and sugar. Add the haricots verts and toss them with tongs to coat them in the Vegan Magic mixture.

Remove the bacon from the air fryer basket. Carefully dice the bacon. Add the bacon to the pan and toss with the haricots verts. Cook at 390°F for 4 minutes.

Serves 4

No-Oil Option: Use vegetable broth instead of the Vegan Magic (keeping in mind that caramelization is less likely).

Baked Spaghetti

Raise your hand if you often find yourself in a pasta rut (my hand is waving in the air). This is a fun way to make a regular old spaghetti dinner a bit more exciting.

4 ounces thin spaghetti
1 teaspoon extra-virgin olive oil
8 ounces vegan beef crumbles
1/4 cup finely chopped onion
2 cloves garlic, minced
1 teaspoon dried oregano
1 teaspoon dried basil
1 to 2 spritzes extra-virgin olive oil
1 (15-ounce) jar marinara sauce
1 cup nondairy shredded mozzarella cheese

Cook the spaghetti in a large saucepan of boiling water until it is al dente, about 8 minutes. Drain and set aside.

Heat the oil in a large skillet over low heat. Add the crumbles, onion, garlic, oregano, and basil. Sauté until the crumbles are heated through, 5 to 7 minutes.

Spritz an air fryer–safe dish that fits into the air fryer with the oil. Transfer half of the spaghetti to the dish. Add half of the crumbles, half of the marinara sauce, and half of the cheese. Add the remaining spaghetti, remaining crumbles, another layer of marinara sauce, and the remaining cheese. Cook at 350°F for 15 minutes.

Serves 2 to 4

No-Oil Option: Substitute the olive oil with vegetable broth or dry-sauté the vegan beef crumbles.

Note

You may have to use smaller dishes, depending upon the size of your air fryer. Halve the cooked spaghetti and cheese and then layer according to the instructions.

Meat-y Balls

This is a tried-and-true meatball recipe. Any bean will do, but I love Italian cannellini beans, because these meatballs are almost destined for a pasta dish. TVP, which is made from soybeans, adds protein and helps bind the meatballs.

1/2 cup dry TVP
1/2 cup vegetable broth
1 1/2 cups cooked (or canned) cannellini beans, drained and rinsed
1/4 cup ground flaxseed
2 tablespoons sesame seeds
2 tablespoons chickpea flour
1 teaspoon sea salt
2 tablespoons nutritional yeast
1 teaspoon dried basil
1 teaspoon dried thyme
1 teaspoon hot sauce
1 to 2 spritzes canola oil

Place the TVP in a medium bowl and pour the broth over it. Let the TVP rehydrate for 10 minutes. Transfer the TVP to a food processor and add the beans, flaxseed, sesame seeds, flour, salt, nutritional yeast, basil, thyme, and hot sauce. Pulse until the ingredients form a dough-like consistency.

Form meatballs by scooping out about 2 tablespoons of the TVP mixture and rolling them in the palms of your hands.

Spritz the air fryer basket with the oil. Place the meatballs in the basket (you may have to cook more than one batch, depending upon the size of your air fryer). Cook at 360°F for 10 to 12 minutes, shaking halfway through the cooking time.

Makes about 15 meatballs

No-Oil Option: Omit the canola oil; you may want to use tongs to move the meatballs more frequently to avoid sticking.

Baked Chick'n-Style Seitan

Use the Dry Seitan Mix to make your own seitan.

> 1 cup Dry Seitan Mix (page 125)
> 3/4 cup vegan chicken broth
> 1 tablespoon low-sodium tamari
> 1/2 teaspoon canola oil
> 1/2 teaspoon blackstrap molasses
> 1 to 2 spritzes vegetable oil spray

Pour the dry seitan mix into a stand mixer bowl.

In a small bowl, combine the broth, tamari, canola oil, and molasses.

Fit the stand mixer with the dough hook and turn the mixer on low. Slowly add the broth mixture to the dry seitan mix. Increase the speed of the stand mixer to high and knead the seitan for 5 minutes.

Grease a 7-inch baking pan with 1 to 2 spritzes of vegetable oil. Press the seitan into the pan. (If this is too large for your air fryer, find an appropriately sized oven-safe pan. You may have to cook the seitan in two batches.) Cover the baking pan with foil.

Place the pan in the air fryer. Cook at 350°F for 10 minutes. Remove the pan from the air fryer, uncover, flip the seitan with a spatula, and cover the pan again. Cook 10 minutes longer.

Serves 4

Dry Seitan Mix

This recipe is designed to help you prepare seitan in bulk. In this case, I don't mean making a bunch and freezing it. Remember, our air fryers aren't huge! Instead, this is a recipe for four cups of the dry ingredients required to make seitan. One cup dry mix combined with the wet ingredients equals one meal. By starting with this formula, you can use it 1 cup at a time and store some in the refrigerator for next time!

3 cups vital wheat gluten
1/2 cup chickpea flour
1/4 cup nutritional yeast
4 teaspoons vegan chicken seasoning
1 teaspoon garlic powder
1 teaspoon freshly ground black pepper

Combine the gluten, flour, nutritional yeast, chicken seasoning, garlic powder, and pepper in a large bowl.

Transfer the mixture to an airtight container, such as a large mason jar, and store it in the refrigerator for up to 3 months.

Makes 4 cups seitan mix

General Tso's Soy Curls

Here's another Asian sauce recipe that's easy to make and tastes delicious on Soy Curls and tofu (make Basic Air-Fried Tofu on page 103 and then toss it in this sauce). I love serving this recipe over brown rice or rolled up in a tortilla for an Asian-style wrap.

2 cups warm vegan chicken broth
2 cups dry Soy Curls
1 teaspoon avocado oil or canola oil
1 teaspoon Tofuna Fysh Sauce (page 11) or 1 teaspoon low-sodium soy sauce mixed with 1/4
  teaspoon dulse flakes
1/4 teaspoon ground ginger
2 1/2 teaspoons potato starch, divided
2 teaspoons brown rice flour or chickpea flour
3 tablespoons soy sauce or tamari
3 tablespoons granulated sugar
2 tablespoons mirin (or increase rice vinegar by 2 tablespoons)
1 1/2 tablespoons rice vinegar
1 tablespoon chili paste
1 tablespoon sesame seeds
Cooked brown rice or noodles, for serving
1/4 cup finely chopped scallions

In a large bowl, pour the warm broth over the Soy Curls. Let the Soy Curls rehydrate for 10 minutes. Drain the Soy Curls in a colander, gently squeezing out excess broth with tongs, and transfer them back to the large bowl. Add the oil, Tofuna Fysh Sauce, ginger, 1 teaspoon of the potato starch, and flour. Toss gently with tongs to coat.

Transfer the Soy Curls to the air fryer basket. Cook at 390°F for 8 minutes, shaking halfway through the cooking time.

While the Soy Curls are in the air fryer, combine the soy sauce, sugar, mirin, vinegar, chili paste, and the remaining 1 1/2 teaspoons potato starch in a medium saucepan over medium-high heat. Stir well.

As soon as the sauce reaches a rolling boil, reduce the heat to low, cover, and simmer while the Soy Curls finish cooking.

Once the Soy Curls are cooked, transfer them to the saucepan. Toss gently to coat with the sauce, cover, and simmer for 3 minutes. Remove the lid from the saucepan, sprinkle the sesame seeds over the Soy Curls and toss one more time. Serve over rice or noodles and garnish with the scallions.

Serves 4

No-Oil Option: Omit the avocado oil.

Chick'n-Fried Steak

The idea of fried steak doesn't sound very healthy and certainly not vegan. However, air-frying battered seitan is a great way to enjoy such comfort food. For added comfort, serve it with mashed or roasted potatoes and Mushroom White Bean Gravy (page 94). Remember that Dry Seitan Mix you made? Now's the time to use it!

1 cup Dry Seitan Mix (page 125)
3/4 cup vegan chicken broth
1 tablespoon low-sodium tamari
1/2 teaspoon canola oil
1/2 teaspoon blackstrap molasses
1 to 2 spritzes vegetable oil
1/2 cup soymilk or other nondairy milk
3 tablespoons barbecue sauce
3 tablespoons chickpea flour
1 cup unbleached all-purpose flour
1/4 cup nutritional yeast
2 tablespoons cornmeal
1 teaspoon garlic powder
1/2 teaspoon sea salt
1/4 teaspoon black pepper

Pour the dry seitan mix into a stand mixer bowl.

In a small bowl, combine the broth, tamari, canola oil, and molasses.

Fit the stand mixer with the dough hook and turn the mixer on low. Slowly add the broth mixture to the dry seitan mix. Increase the speed of the mixer to high and knead the seitan for 5 minutes.

Spray a 7 x 7 x 3-inch baking pan with 1 to 2 spritzes of vegetable oil spray. Press the seitan into the prepared pan. (If this size pan is too large for your air fryer, find an appropriately sized oven-safe pan. You may have to cook the seitan in two batches.) Cover the baking pan with foil.

Place the pan in the air fryer. Cook at 350°F for 10 minutes. Remove the pan from the air fryer, uncover, flip the seitan with a spatula, and cover the pan again. Cook for 10 minutes longer. Remove the seitan from the air fryer and set aside.

In a medium bowl, combine the milk, barbecue sauce, and chickpea flour in a medium bowl.

In a small bowl, combine the all-purpose flour, nutritional yeast, cornmeal, garlic powder, salt, and pepper. Transfer half the all-purpose flour mixture to an airtight container and half to a shallow dish for dredging.

Preheat the air fryer to 370°F for 3 minutes. Once the seitan is cool enough to touch, slice it into 4 pieces.

Dip each piece of seitan into the milk mixture. Then dredge the seitan through the all-purpose flour mixture. If necessary, add more of the all-purpose flour mixture from the airtight container (otherwise, store any remaining all-purpose flour mixture in the refrigerator for future use). Do not discard the milk mixture after all the seitan pieces are battered.

Cook the battered seitan at 370°F for 2 minutes. Flip the seitan with tongs and cook for 2 more minutes. Remove the chik'n-fried steaks from the air fryer and dip them back into the remaining milk mixture, flipping them to coat both sides. Return the chik'n-fried steaks to the air fryer and cook for 3 more minutes.

Serves 4

No-Oil Option: Omit the canola oil in the seitan and do not spritz the air fryer with vegetable oil.

Chick'n Pot Pie

Here's a fun way to use Fried Biscuits (page 27). (If you're short on time, you use a tube of prepared biscuits instead.) This recipe is versatile. You can use any number of vegan chicken strips, which are often sold in the frozen foods section of the grocery store, but consider using Soy Curls or Baked Chick'n-Style Seitan (page 124) instead. This beautiful, comforting bowl will be on the table in thirty minutes. And this is the kind of dish to serve to nonvegan family members or friends!

> Fried Biscuits dough (page 27) or one (16-ounce) tube prepared vegan biscuits
> 1 teaspoon extra-virgin olive oil (optional)
> 2 cloves garlic, minced
> 1 cup finely chopped onion
> 1/2 cup finely chopped carrot
> 1/2 cup coarsely chopped celery
> 1 teaspoon dried thyme
> 1/2 teaspoon sea salt
> 1/4 teaspoon black pepper
> 4 ounces vegan chicken strips, thawed if frozen
> 1 cup Mushroom White Bean Gravy (page 94) or Pacific brand or Imagine brand vegan mushroom gravy

Prepare half of the biscuit dough and set aside (don't bake it).

Heat the oil in a large skillet over medium heat. Add the garlic, onion, carrot, celery, thyme, salt, and pepper and cook for 5 to 8 minutes, until the carrots are tender with a slight crunch.

Coarsely chop the chicken strips and add them to the skillet. Pour the gravy into the skillet, stir, and bring the mixture to a boil. Cover, reduce the heat to low, and simmer for 10 minutes.

Divide the pot pie mixture between 2 (5-inch diameter) ramekins or baking pans.

Preheat the air fryer to 360° for 5 minutes. If you are using the fried biscuit dough, divide the dough in half. Using your hands, flatten out 2 pieces of dough to go over each ramekin. If using store-bought biscuits, you will need a total of 4 biscuits. Using your hands, combine 2 biscuits and flatten them out into a dough to cover a ramekin. Repeat this process to create a second piece of dough for the other ramekin.

Take 1 biscuit dough half and cover a ramekin. Crimp the dough around the edge of the ramekin to completely cover the pot pie mixture. Repeat this process with the other half of the biscuit dough and the other ramekin.

Place the ramekins in the air fryer. (You may have to prepare one pot pie at a time, depending upon the size of your air fryer; if so, place the first cooked pot pie in a warm oven while cooking the second.)

Cook the pot pies at 360°F for 8 minutes, until golden brown. Use silcone gloves or hot pads with a spatula to carefully remove the pot pies from the air fryer.

Serves 2

No-Oil Option: Use vegetable broth or water to sauté the vegetables.

7

One-pot meals are all the rage. Whether you're in the mood for a hearty stew cooked on the stove, a rice and bean dish made in a pressure cooker or Instant Pot, or even a veggie-filled porridge in a rice cooker, you can throw everything into one pot and be done with it. This chapter is devoted to getting lunch or dinner on the table fast, with no fuss and only a little mess.

One-Basket Meals

Fried Tacos

While I was growing up along the Mississippi River in rural Iowa, we frequented several tiny mom-and-pop Mexican restaurants. It wasn't until I moved on to a big city that I learned that most people don't fry their tacos. What? No deep-fried tacos? With an air fryer, I'm able to get the texture and flavors I grew up with without all the deep-fryer fat. If you can't find seasoned crumbles, combine plain vegan beef crumbles or rehydrated TVP with 1/2 cup salsa.

4 (6-inch) flour tortillas
4 spritzes canola oil spray
2 cups frozen vegan seasoned beef crumbles (such as Beyond Meat Feisty Crumble)
1 cup shredded nondairy cheddar or pepper Jack cheese
2 cups shredded lettuce
1 cup finely chopped tomatoes
1/2 cup finely chopped onion

Preheat the air fryer to 360°F for 3 minutes. Place a stainless steel taco holder in the air fryer.

Spritz one side of the tortillas with canola oil. Insert the tortillas into the taco holder, oiled side out. Scoop 1/2 cup beef crumbles into each tortilla. Add 1/4 cup cheese to each tortilla.

Cook at 360°F for 8 minutes.

Remove the taco stand from the air fryer with tongs. Garnish each taco with 1/2 cup of lettuce, 1/4 cup of tomatoes, and 2 tablespoons of onion.

Makes 4 tacos

No-Oil Option: Omit the canola oil spray (but note that the result will not be the puffy taco this recipe aims for).

Note

If you don't have a taco holder, arrange several tacos side by side, from one wall of the air fryer basket to the other, to hold them upright. Or simply fill the soft tortillas and place them on their side, leaning against each other in the basket. You might use a toothpick to keep all the good stuff inside each taco.

Gourmet Grilled Cheese

A gourmet sandwich in an air fryer? Sure! It just requires attention to a few details. You can use store-bought bread or bake the bread yourself. I recommend Kite Hill Chive Cream Cheese Style Spread or Miyoko's Kitchen Classic Double Cream Chive.

1 small Anjou or Asian pear (or any juicy, soft pear)

1 small Vidalia or sweet onion

1/4 teaspoon sugar

1/2 to 1 teaspoon extra-virgin olive oil or nondairy butter

1/2 cup nondairy cream cheese

4 slices sourdough bread or other crusty bread

2 to 4 spritzes extra-virgin olive oil

Cut the pear lengthwise into thin slices. Cut the onion into thin half-moon slices. Place the pear, onion, and sugar on a piece of foil. Drizzle the oil over (or place the butter on) the pear and onion. Loosely wrap the foil around the pear and onion. Place the foil pouch in the air basket fryer. Cook at 390°F for 15 minutes. Remove the foil pouch from the air fryer with tongs or a spatula, open the foil to release the steam, and set aside.

Spread 2 tablespoons cream cheese on 1 slice of the bread. Using tongs, place half of the caramelized pear and onion on top of the cream cheese. Spread another 2 tablespoons cream cheese on another slice of bread. Place this slice of bread on top of the pear and onion. Repeat this process to make the second sandwich. Spray the air fryer basket with the oil. Place the sandwiches in the air fryer. Spritz the top of the bread with more oil. Cook at 390°F for 5 to 7 minutes, until the bread is golden brown.

Serves 2

No-Oil Option: Omit the olive oil.

Note

If you have a smaller air fryer, you may have to make the sandwiches one at a time.

Roasted Chickpeas and Broccoli

Bowl meals are a favorite in my household, as they almost always allow you to work with three of the five vegan food groups (vegetables, fruit, legumes, grains, and nuts and seeds). This dish starts with vegetables and beans in the air fryer. Serve it with sesame seeds or, to counter the roasted crunch, opt for the Peanut Sauce on page 59.

1 (15-ounce) can chickpeas, drained, rinsed, and patted dry
1/2 cup thin half-moon onion slices
1 teaspoon canola oil
1 teaspoon low-sodium soy sauce
1 teaspoon ground ginger
1/2 teaspoon granulated garlic
1/2 teaspoon black pepper
1/2 teaspoon curry powder
2 cups broccoli florets
1 tablespoon sesame seeds, for serving

Combine the chickpeas, onion, oil, and soy sauce in a large bowl. Add the ginger, granulated garlic, pepper, and curry powder and toss until all chickpeas are well coated.

Transfer the chickpeas to the air fryer basket using a slotted spoon (to reserve the oil and soy sauce marinade). Cook at 390°F for 7 minutes, shaking at 5 minutes.

In a large bowl, combine the broccoli with the leftover marinade. Transfer to the air fryer after the chickpeas and onion have cooked for 7 minutes. Gently toss the broccoli with the chickpeas and onion. Continue cooking at 390°F for another 5 minutes, shaking halfway through the cooking time, until the broccoli is tender but retains a slight crunch.

Sprinkle 1/2 tablespoon of sesame seeds over each serving.

Serves 2

No-Oil Option: Omit the canola oil.

Seitan Fajitas

Here's some great news, air-frying enthusiasts! You can "stir-fry" in an air fryer. The result is food with a good bit of crunch, which is particularly delicious in soft tortillas.

8 ounces Baked Chick'n-Style Seitan (page 124), cut into 1/2-inch thick strips or store-bought seitan strips
1 large red bell pepper, cut into 1/4-inch thick strips
1 large green bell pepper, cut into 1/4-inch thick strips
1 medium onion, cut into 1/4-inch thick half-moon slices
3 cloves garlic, coarsely chopped
1 teaspoon canola oil
1/2 teaspoon chili powder
1/2 teaspoon ground cumin
1/2 teaspoon paprika
1/4 teaspoon sea salt
1/4 teaspoon black pepper
4 (12-inch) flour tortillas

Place the seitan slices in a large bowl (if using packaged seitan, drain before adding to the bowl). Add the red bell pepper, green bell pepper, onion, and garlic to the bowl with the seitan. Drizzle the oil over the seitan and vegetables and toss with tongs to coat. Add the chili powder, cumin, paprika, salt, and pepper, tossing to combine.

Transfer the mixture to the air fryer basket. Cook at 370°F for 10 to 12 minutes, shaking halfway through the cooking time.

Warm the tortillas in the oven or microwave.

Assemble the fajitas by placing one-fourth of the seitan and vegetables in each tortilla.

Serves 4

No-Oil Option: Omit the canola oil.

Taco Salad

I've never been one to fix it if it ain't broke, so let's try a salad version of the fried tacos, this time with seitan and beans. An air fryer–safe tortilla-shell maker accessory (see page 3) is required to turn the tortillas into salad bowls.

4 (8-inch) flour tortillas
8 ounces Baked Chick'n-Style Seitan (page 124) or store-bought seitan, coarsely chopped
1 (15-ounce) can pinto beans, drained and rinsed
3/4 cup salsa
1/2 cup finely chopped onion
1 cup shredded nondairy cheddar cheese
2 cups finely shredded lettuce
1 cup finely chopped tomatoes

Press the tortillas into shell molds. Set aside.

Place the seitan in a medium bowl. Add the beans, salsa, and onion. Combine well.

Divide the seitan mixture between the tortillas. It's likely you will only be able to make 2 taco salads at one time in a large air fryer and 1 in a small air fryer. Turn the oven on to warm to heat each taco salad as it comes out of the air fryer.

Place as many tortilla shells into the air fryer as will fit. Cook at 360°F for 5 minutes.

Add 1/2 cup cheese to each tortilla. Cook at 360°F for 2 minutes longer. Transfer the cooked tortilla bowls to the oven to warm while cooking the next set.

When all the tortilla bowls are cooked, gently use tongs to slide them from the tortilla-shell mold to a serving plate. Add 1 cup shredded lettuce and 1/2 cup tomatoes to each taco salad.

Serves 4

Tempeh Fried Rice

Because traditional fried rice made in an air fryer is tricky (because the rice falls through the basket openings), this version has a hearty, sticky texture. This recipe calls for a vegan egg. In this case, the Follow Your Heart brand egg replacer is the only one that meets my standards.

8 ounces tempeh
1/2 cup coarsely chopped shiitake mushrooms
1/2 cup plus 1 tablespoon low-sodium soy sauce, divided
2 tablespoons maple syrup
1 teaspoon extra-virgin olive oil
2 cloves garlic, minced
1/2 cup ice cold water
2 tablespoons Follow Your Heart VeganEgg
1/4 teaspoon black salt
1 1/2 cups cooked brown rice
2 tablespoons nutritional yeast
1 cup bean sprouts
1 cup shredded cabbage
1 teaspoon chili paste

Steam the tempeh for 10 minutes in a medium saucepan on the stove (or for 1 minute on low pressure in an Instant Pot or pressure cooker; use a quick release). Dice the tempeh into 12 pieces and transfer it to a shallow dish. Add the mushrooms.

In a small bowl, whisk together 1/2 cup of the soy sauce, maple syrup, oil, and garlic. Pour the marinade over the tempeh and mushrooms. Cover the dish with foil and set aside to marinate for at least 30 minutes (or up to overnight).

Preheat the air fryer to 390°F for 5 minutes. Pulse the water, VeganEgg, and black salt together in a blender. Transfer the marinated tempeh and mushrooms to a nonstick air fryer pan or baking pan that will fit in your air fryer. Add the cooked rice to the pan. Pour the VeganEgg mixture over the rice. Add the nutritional yeast, sprouts, cabbage, remaining 1 tablespoon soy sauce, and chili paste. Mix well and pat the rice down. Cook at 390°F for 10 minutes, tossing the rice mixture with tongs halfway through the cooking time.

Serves 4

No-Oil Option: Omit the olive oil.

Soy Curl Kimchee Spring Rolls

Remember those Soy Curl Fries? They are perfect in this simple spring roll. The Korean condiment is a fermented food that brings in an umami element. I encourage you to make your own variations with your favorite raw vegetables, such as strips of bell pepper, zucchini, or cucumber.

1 cup Soy Curl Fries (page 43) or vegan frozen chicken strips
1 small carrot
4 fresh basil leaves
1/2 cup homemade or store-bought vegan kimchee
4 (6 to 8 1/2-inch) rice paper sheets
2 to 3 spritzes canola oil

Prepare the Soy Curl Fries. If you are using vegan chicken strips, thaw them and cut them in half lengthwise.

Cut the carrot into matchsticks and divide the matchsticks into fourths.

Dip 1 sheet of rice paper in warm water for 5 seconds or until moistened. Place the moist rice paper on a work surface and let sit for 30 seconds or until pliable. Place 1 basil leaf on the rice paper. Add one-fourth of the carrot matchsticks, 2 tablespoons kimchee, and 1/4 cup Soy Curl Fries.

Roll the rice paper by pulling the edge away from the cutting board. Roll over the filling while gathering and tucking the filling under the wrapper, rolling until you come to the end of the paper. Repeat this process until you have created 4 spring rolls.

Spray 1 to 2 spritzes canola oil on the air fryer basket. Place the spring rolls in the air fryer basket and spritz the top of the rolls with the remaining 1 to 2 spritzes oil. Cook at 400°F for 6 minutes, shaking halfway through the cooking time.

Makes 4 spring rolls

No-Oil Option: Omit the the canola oil.

Lasagna Casserole

In this lasagna, the noodles are vegetables. They cook beautifully in a 7-inch baking pan that is about 3 inches high. If you have a smaller air fryer, use an air fryer—safe dish that fits—in that case, don't worry about layering everything beautifully. It's going to taste the same!

1 small zucchini
1 small yellow squash
1 medium onion
1 large red bell pepper
5 ounces nondairy buffalo-style mozzarella cheese
1/4 cup sliced pitted oil-cured black olives
1 teaspoon dried basil
1 teaspoon sea salt
1/2 teaspoon dried oregano
1/4 teaspoon red pepper flakes
1/4 teaspoon ground black pepper
1 (15-ounce) can tomato sauce
1/4 cup shredded nondairy Parmesan cheese

Slice the zucchini and yellow squash lengthwise into 1/8- to 1/4-inch thick strips. Divide both into two parts.

Cut the onion into half-moon slices. Divide the slices into three parts. Cut the bell pepper lengthwise into 1 1/2-inch strips. Divide the strips into three parts.

Cut the mozzarella into 1/4-inch cubes. Transfer the cubes to a small bowl and add the olives, basil, salt, oregano, red pepper flakes, and pepper. Combine well and divide the mixture into three parts.

Preheat the air fryer to 360°F for 5 minutes. Spread 1/2 cup of the tomato sauce into the bottom of a 6 to 7-inch baking pan. Layer one part each of zuchinni, squash, onion, and pepper on top of the tomato sauce. Add the first third of the mozzarella mixture. Repeat this process for 2 more layers. Sprinkle the top layer with the Parmesan.

Cover the baking pan with foil, transfer to the air fryer, and cook at 360°F for 15 minutes. Uncover and cook for 10 more minutes.

Serves 2 to 4

Potatoes, Brussels Sprouts, and Soy Curls

This recipe allows you to layer the air fryer basket with foods that require different cooking times. For example, potatoes require the longest cooking time, so they go in first. You can prep the Brussels sprouts while the potatoes cook, and so on. This allows you to cook and prep simultaneously, getting the meal ready in twenty-eight short minutes.

1 large russet potato, cut into 1/2-inch cubes
1 1/2 teaspoons canola oil, divided
1/2 teaspoon sea salt
1/4 teaspoon black pepper
2 cups dry Soy Curls
2 cups warm water
16 ounces Brussels sprouts, trimmed and halved lengthwise
1 teaspoon balsamic vinegar
1 1/2 teaspoons vegan beef bouillon granules
1 teaspoon ground cumin
1 teaspoon chili powder
1 teaspoon dried dill
1 tablespoon chickpea flour
1 tablespoon cornstarch

Toss the potato in 1/2 teaspoon of the oil, salt, and pepper and transfer to the air fryer. Cook at 400°F for 10 minutes. In a medium bowl, rehydrate the Soy Curls in the warm water for 10 minutes. In a medium bowl, toss the Brussels sprouts with 1/2 teaspoon of the canola oil and the vinegar. When the air fryer beeps at 10 minutes, transfer the Brussels sprouts to the air fryer with the potatoes. Shake and cook at 400°F for 3 minutes.

Drain the Soy Curls, transfer them back to the bowl and toss them with the bouillon granules, cumin, chili powder, dill, chickpea flour, cornstarch, and remaining 1/2 teaspoon canola oil. When the air fryer beeps after 3 minutes, transfer the coated Soy Curls to the basket with the potatoes and Brussels sprouts. Shake and set the timer for 15 minutes. Shake every 5 minutes.

Serves 4

No-Oil Option: Omit the canola oil.

Calzone

I love making this recipe because it looks so beautiful right out of the air fryer—remember that we do eat with our eyes first. Place the calzone on a serving platter and wow your nonvegan friends and family.

4 ounces prepared Pizza Dough (page 14) or store-bought vegan pizza dough
1/4 cup shredded nondairy mozzarella cheese
1/4 cup sliced mushrooms
1/4 cup sliced onion
2 ounces vegan Italian-style seitan crumbles or vegan pepperoni
1/4 cup pizza sauce
1/2 teaspoon dried oregano
1/2 teaspoon dried basil
1/2 cup loosely packed baby spinach leaves
2 to 3 spritzes extra-virgin olive oil or canola oil

Allow the pizza dough to come to room temperature. Hand-press or roll out the dough to about 10 inches.

If using a grill insert, place it inside the air fryer. Preheat the air fryer to 390°F.

Assemble layers on one half of the rolled dough. Start with the cheese, then add the mushrooms, onion, seitan crumbles, pizza sauce, oregano, basil, and spinach. Flip the other half of the dough over the filling. Crimp the edges by pulling the bottom layer of dough over the top layer.

Cut three small slices on the top portion of dough to vent. Spritz the grill insert or the air fryer basket with the oil. Use a large spatula to transfer the calzone to the air fryer basket. Spritz the top of the calzone with additional oil.

Cook at 390°F for 7 to 8 minutes, until the crust is golden brown. Slide the calzone onto a cutting board or serving platter. Slice into 2 pieces and serve.

Serves 2

Note

If you have a small air fryer, consider making two smaller calzones; you may have to cook in two batches.

Fried Sushi Rolls

Many people think sushi is synonymous with raw fish. Actually, sushi rolls consist of seasoned rice in combination with the filling of your choice (in this case, vegetables), all wrapped up in a nori (seaweed) sheet. Thanks to my air fryer and rice paper, I now enjoy making hot, crunchy homemade sushi rolls. (Remember, you can find rice paper online, at the Asian market, or in the ethnic aisle of many grocery stores.)

4 (6 to 8 1/2-inch) sheets rice paper
4 (8 x 7-inch) sheets nori
1/4 cup room-temperature cooked sushi rice
1/4 cup thawed edamame
1 cup thinly sliced red bell pepper, carrot, and jicama
1 to 2 spritzes avocado oil or extra-virgin olive oil

Dip 1 sheet of the rice paper in warm water for about 5 seconds or until moistened. Place the moist rice paper on a work surface and let sit for 30 seconds or until pliable.

Place 1 nori sheet on the wet rice paper. Spoon 1 tablespoon sushi rice onto the nori sheet, making a line with the rice. Spoon 1 tablespoon edamame onto the nori sheet beside the rice, forming another line. Assemble 1/4 cup of the sliced vegetable mixture alongside the rice and edamame.

Roll the rice paper by pulling the edge away from the cutting board. Roll over the filling while gathering and tucking the nori sheet and filling under the rice paper, rolling until you come to the end of the paper. Repeat this process until you have created 4 rolls.

Place the rolls in the air fryer basket. Spritz the rolls with the oil. Cook at 390°F for 5 minutes, shaking halfway through the cooking time.

Serves 4

No-Oil Option: Omit the avocado oil.

8

*D*essert just got a lot easier with an air fryer. Simple ingredients plus rapid cooking equals sweet treats fast. My savory tooth is far more dominant than my sweet tooth, so you might want to amp up the sugary ingredients. You'll also find that many of these recipes could easily stand in for a sweet breakfast. It's just one of the many perks of cooking vegan, right?

So Sweet

Fruit Crumble

Not a baker, I discovered this simple way to prepare a warm fruit dessert or snack many years ago. I'm particularly fond of it because having leftovers of a fruit crumble is never an issue. Make what you want to eat!

1 medium apple, finely diced
1/2 cup frozen blueberries, strawberries, or peaches
1/4 cup plus 1 tablespoon brown rice flour
2 tablespoons sugar
1/2 teaspoon ground cinnamon
2 tablespoons nondairy butter

Preheat the air fryer to 350°F for 5 minutes.

Combine the apple and frozen blueberries in an air fryer–safe baking pan or ramekin.

In a small bowl, combine the flour, sugar, cinnamon, and butter. Spoon the flour mixture over the fruit. Sprinkle a little extra flour over everything to cover any exposed fruit. Cook at 350°F for 15 minutes.

Serves 2

Cake for One

This is a fun little treat when you're craving chocolate. Serve with a small dollop of nondairy ice cream or the Simple Coco Whip.

3 tablespoons unbleached all-purpose flour
1 1/2 tablespoons cocoa powder
1 tablespoon plus 1 teaspoon sugar
1/4 teaspoon baking powder
1/8 teaspoon salt
3 teaspoons applesauce
3 tablespoons almond milk
1/2 teaspoon vanilla extract
1 to 2 spritzes canola oil
Simple Coco Whip (page 157), for serving (optional)

In a medium bowl, combine the flour, cocoa powder, sugar, baking powder, and salt.

In a small bowl, combine the applesauce, milk, and vanilla. Pour the applesauce mixture over the flour mixture and stir until there are no lumps in the batter.

Spritz a small ramekin or baking pan with the oil (if you are omitting the oil, use a nonstick pan). Pour the batter into the ramekin.

Cook at 360°F for 7 to 10 minutes. The cake is done when you insert a toothpick into the center and it comes out clean. When the cake is cool, serve with the coco whip, if desired.

Serves 1

No-Oil Option: Omit the canola oil.

Simple Coco Whip

For a delicious change of flavor, substitute peppermint or almond extract for the vanilla.

> **1 (13-ounce) can full-fat coconut milk**
> **1 tablespoon sugar**
> **1 teaspoon vanilla extract**

Refrigerate the can of coconut milk overnight.

Open the can and scoop out the solid cream into a stand mixer bowl or mixing bowl if you are using an electric mixer. (Reserve any liquid in the can for another use—it's a great addition to breakfast oats or soups.)

On high-speed, beat the coconut cream until stiff peaks are formed. Add the sugar and vanilla and beat for 1 minute longer. Serve immediately.

Makes about 2 cups

Fruit Cobbler for One

This cobbler-ish sweet treat is pretty wholesome. So why not serve it alongside a scoop of nondairy ice cream? I use my small, 4.6-inch wide cast iron crock, which fits the air fryer nicely. It works great for cooking and also makes for a gorgeous presentation.

1/2 cup chopped frozen peaches or blueberries
1/2 cup granola or muesli
1/2 teaspoon cold nondairy butter, cut into small cubes

Layer the peaches, granola, and butter in a small air fryer–safe casserole dish. Cover the dish with a heatproof lid or foil.

Cook at 390°F for 6 minutes. Remove the cover and cook at 390°F for 2 minutes longer.

Serves 1

Bread Pudding

Here's a dessert that could easily stand in for breakfast. Mix up the dried fruit and nuts: cranberries, cherries, and pecans turn it into a festive holiday dish.

2 cups cubed day-old bread (a French baguette or sourdough bread is ideal)
1 1/2 cups soymilk
1 tablespoon sugar
1/4 teaspoon vanilla extract
1/2 teaspoon ground cinnamon
1/4 cup golden raisins
1/4 cup dried currants
1/4 cup finely chopped walnuts

Preheat the air fryer to 360°F for 3 minutes. Place the bread in a medium bowl.

In a small bowl, combine the milk, sugar, vanilla, cinnamon, raisins, currants, and walnuts. Pour the milk mixture over the bread and mix well. Transfer the mixture to a nonstick, air fryer–safe baking pan that fits into the basket (for smaller air fryers, divide the bread mixture between 2 small dishes, such as ramekins).

Cook at 360°F for 20 minutes. Remove the bread pudding from the air fryer and let it cool for 20 to 30 minutes before serving.

Serves 4

Fruit Pastry Pockets

I'm a savory gal, so this recipe hits the spot—for me. If you're a fan of sweet treats, sprinkle 1 to 2 teaspoons sugar over the crescent roll dough before rolling it out.

> 4 ounces vegan crescent roll dough
> 1 tablespoon unbleached all-purpose flour
> 6 ounces fresh blueberries, strawberries, or blackberries
> 1/2 teaspoon granulated sugar
> 1/4 teaspoon ground cardamom
> 1/4 teaspoon ground ginger
> 1 teaspoon powdered sugar

Divide the crescent roll dough into 4 equal parts. Sprinkle the flour on a work surface and roll the dough pieces out to 5 x 5-inch pieces, using more flour as needed to avoid sticking.

In a medium bowl, combine the blueberries, sugar, cardamom, and ginger.

Preheat the air fryer to 360°F for 4 minutes. Spoon about 1/3 cup of the blueberry mixture onto each piece of dough. Fold each corner toward the center. Work the edges of the dough to ensure it's sealed; it will resemble a pocket. Cook at 360°F for 6 to 7 minutes, or until golden brown.

Sprinkle the powdered sugar on the pastry pockets before serving.

Makes 4

Roasted Cherries Jubilee

With just three ingredients and only ten minutes in the air fryer, this simple fruit topping is great over nondairy ice cream or mixed with granola. And—back to breakfast—it's fantastic over a bowl of hot steel-cut oatmeal.

2 tablespoons nondairy butter
2 cups fresh cherries, pitted and halved
2 tablespoons sugar

Melt the butter in a microwave.

In a medium bowl, toss the cherries with the butter and sugar.

Transfer the cherries to a small baking pan and place it in the air fryer basket.

Cook at 350°F for 10 minutes, shaking halfway through the cooking time. Transfer the cherries to a bowl and allow them to cool.

Serves 2 to 4

Baked Apples

With a nod to tradition, the ingredients for these baked apples are simple: apples, brown sugar, butter, and cinnamon. Of course, this healthier approach uses nondairy butter and less sugar, and I've added rolled oats for fiber and flavor.

1/2 cup rolled oats
1 teaspoon brown sugar
1 tablespoon nondairy butter, softened
1 tablespoon coarsely chopped pecans
1 teaspoon ground cinnamon
4 large Granny Smith or other baking apples, cored

Preheat the air fryer to 360°F for 5 minutes.

In a small bowl, combine the oats, brown sugar, butter, pecans, and cinnamon.

Using a small spoon, fill the apples with the oat mixture. Cook at 360°F for 20 to 25 minutes.

Serves 4

Note

Good news! If your apples begin to crumble when coring, you can either chop the apple pieces and add them to the oat filling or dice them up and use the extra oat mixture to make a quickie crumble in an oven-safe pan: simply cook it at 360°F for 15 minutes.

Caramelized Fruit-and-Nut Topping

A sweet and savory caramelized treat turns the ordinary into the extraordinary. Serve over blended frozen bananas, chopped fresh fruit or, for a non-dessert option, over a salad or in a Roasted Acorn Squash half (page 78).

1 teaspoon sugar
1 teaspoon light agave syrup
1 teaspoon nondairy butter
1/2 cup coarsely chopped walnuts
1/2 cup coarsely chopped pecans
1/2 cup coarsely chopped dried apricots, cherries, cranberries, or raisins
1/4 teaspoon ground cinnamon

Combine the sugar, agave syrup, and butter in an air fryer–safe baking pan. Heat the pan in the air fryer for 2 minutes at 360°F. Remove from the air fryer.

Add the walnuts, pecans, apricots, and cinnamon. Toss to coat. Return the pan to the air fryer basket. Cook at 390°F for 5 minutes, stirring at 3 minutes.

Makes 1 1/2 cups

Fried Ginger-O's

If you're like me, you've spent some time at state fairs. For all kinds of reasons, they're not exactly vegan friendly, am I right? No event can serve up fried food like a big Midwest festival—they even fry Oreos! Here's a fun vegan version. If you can't find Newman's Own brand sandwich cookies, you can always turn to Oreos, which are accidentally made with plant-based ingredients.

> 3/4 cup vegan instant pancake mix
> 2/3 cup water
> 1/4 cup soy flour
> 1/8 teaspoon vanilla extract
> 1/2 teaspoon sugar
> 8 Newman's Own Ginger-O's sandwich cookies (or Newman's Own O cookie flavor of your choice or traditional Oreos)

Preheat the air fryer to 390°F for 5 minutes. Place a piece of parchment paper on the air fryer basket; just enough to cover the bottom and with no excess exposed.

In a large bowl, combine the pancake mix, water, soy flour, vanilla, and sugar, whisking well.

Dip the cookies into the batter one at a time with tongs. Shake excess batter off and transfer the cookies to the air fryer basket. You may have to do this in batches, based on the size of your air fryer.

Cook at 390°F for 5 minutes. Flip the cookies over, removing the parchment paper. Cook for 2 to 3 more minutes. The cookies are done when they are golden brown.

Makes 8 cookies

Note

Good news! You can double this recipe and make more cookies. After air-frying them, let them cool. Then wrap them in parchment paper and store in an airtight container or in a freezer bag. Next time you're ready to eat one (or two or three) simply air-fry them, frozen, at 390°F for 4 minutes.

Apple Pie Taquitos

These taquitos are embarassingly easy. You can start with a can of pie filling and finish up with a sprinkle of cinnamon. Or you can take an extra step and make the Chunky Applesauce for a special filling, which is what I highly recommend.

> 2 to 3 spritzes canola oil
> 1/4 cup apple pie filling or Chunky Applesauce (follows)
> 2 (6-inch) corn tortillas
> 1 teaspoon ground cinnamon, divided

Spritz the air fryer basket with the oil.

Spread 2 tablespoons pie filling onto 1 tortilla. Roll the tortilla up and place it in the air fryer basket. Repeat this process to create the second taquito. Spritz more oil on the top of the tortillas. Sprinkle 1/2 teaspoon of the cinnamon over the taquitos. Cook at 390°F for 4 minutes. Turn the taquitos over, sprinkle the remaining 1/2 teasoon cinnamon over the taquitos and cook for 1 minute longer.

Makes 2 taquitos

No-Oil Option: Omit the canola oil.

Chunky Applesauce

> 1 large Granny Smith apple, cored, quartered, and cut into 1/2-inch pieces
> 1/2 teaspoon ground ginger
> 1/2 teaspoon ground cinnamon
> 1/4 to 1/2 cup water

Stovetop Method: Combine the apple, ginger, and cinnamon in a medium saucepan. Stir in 1/4 cup water. Bring to a boil over medium-high heat. Once the mixture is boiling, cover the saucepan, reduce the heat to low, and let the mixture simmer 15 to 20 minutes. Add up to 1/4 cup more water if needed.

Pressure Cooker or Instant Pot Method: Place the apple in the pot. Add the ginger, cinnamon, and 1/4 cup water. Cover the pressure cooker and bring to pressure (if you are using an Instant Pot, choose

3 minutes at high pressure). Cook at pressure for 3 minutes. Use a quick release. When the apples are tender, mash them with a fork or potato masher.

Makes about 1 cup

Shortbread Cake

My great-grandmother had my Great Uncle Wayne's favorite cookies stored in her freezer at all times. Whenever we would visit (which was constantly, as she lived around the block), we would ask, "Can we have Uncle Wayne's cookies?" I know that in some parts, these treats are referred to as Mexican wedding cookies, pecan sandies, or Russian tea cakes, but they will always be Uncle Wayne's cookies to me. For this recipe, you can spread the dough into a springform pan to create a treat that falls somewhere between a cake and a tart—or you can make the cookies variation.

     1 cup nondairy butter
     1 tablespoon vanilla extract
     2 cups unbleached all-purpose flour, sifted
     1/3 cup powdered sugar, sifted and packed, plus more as needed
     1 cup finely chopped pecans

Cream the butter (I use a stand mixer fitted with the plastic paddle). Add the vanilla and continue mixing. Slowly add the flour, and then the powdered sugar, and mix well. Mix in the pecans.

Shortbread Cake: Roll the dough into a ball. Preheat the air fryer to 330°F for 3 minutes.

Press the dough into the bottom of an 8-inch springform pan (you may have to adjust how many cakes you make with the dough, based on the size of your air fryer). Place the pan in the air fryer and cook at 330°F for 15 to 17 minutes.

Transfer the pan to a baking rack and allow the cake to cool for 20 to 30 minutes. Serve the cake warm with Caramelized Fruit-and-Nut Topping (page 167) or simply dust it with additional powdered sugar.

For Cookies: Preheat the air fryer to 330°F for 3 minutes. Scoop out 2 teaspoons dough and roll into a ball. Set aside. Repeat until you have enough cookies to fill the air fryer basket. (You'll continue forming cookie balls while the first batch cooks.) Bake at 330°F for 12 to 15 minutes, shaking at 6 minutes. While the cookies are still warm, roll each cookie in the powdered sugar and let them cool on a baking rack.

Makes 1 cake or 2 to 3 dozen cookies

Resources

Many of you picked up this book because you are reducing or eliminating oil from your diet. As you can tell from my recipes, I use oil. But you may have health reasons to avoid it. Since this book is a vegan cookbook, and I'm the cook, I turned to my friend Ginny Messina, my coauthor of Vegan for Her: The Woman's Guide to Being Healthy and Fit on a Plant-Based Diet, *to offer her professional opinion on oils. I hope you find it as informative as I do!*

How to Use Oils in a Healthy Vegan Diet

by Virginia Messina, MPH, RD

When JL told me I needed an air fryer, I was skeptical. I don't eat a low-fat diet and I have no particular fear of oil. Why would I need to fry my food in air?

But JL has never steered me wrong, so I decided to give it a try. And the air fryer quickly became my favorite cooking appliance. I use it every day, because while I'm not afraid of oil, the truth is that I don't want to guzzle it by the gallon. The air fryer meets my needs perfectly; it serves up the culinary benefits of cooking with oil in low-oil recipes. I especially love the idea of low-oil foods that remind me of old-fashioned fried favorites.

Over the years, oil has gotten a little bit of a bad rap. In the 1980s and '90s, when low-fat diets were all the rage, there didn't seem to be any place for oil. Nutrition research is ever evolving, though, and the emerging story has put fat-rich foods, including oils, in a whole new light. Now we know that how much fat you eat is far less important than the type you eat. Saturated fat is still off the menu since it raises risk for chronic diseases. But fat from plant foods is actually good for you.

According to the latest evidence, there is a big range of fat intakes that support health. Anywhere from 20 to 35 percent of your calories can come from fat. That's between 45 and 75 grams of fat for someone consuming 2,000 calories per day. It's a big range and it means there is room for everyone—those who prefer to eat a lower fat diet and those of us who enjoy higher-fat plant foods.

When it comes to oil in diets, there are definitely healthy and not-so-healthy ways to use it. Meat and peeled potatoes deep-fried in oil? Not so good. But tomatoes air-roasted with a drizzle of olive oil and a dusting of herbs? Or a few sprays of avocado oil on baked tofu? That's a different story altogether.

While we know that meals packed with certain fats, including fats from plants—well over 3 tablespoons per serving in some studies –can damage the lining of the arteries, meals that use just small amounts of oil have exactly the opposite effect. In Mediterranean populations, adding extra-virgin olive oil to diets reduces risk of dying from a heart attack or stroke, for example.

When we use oil the right way, these modest amounts go a long way toward enhancing flavor and texture of foods and toward helping us create some of the most healthful cuisine in the world. After all, plant-based traditions around the globe use all types of oil in diets that are associated with excellent health.

There are a number of theories about how oil may play a health-promoting role. Just a drizzle of oil makes flavors pop, so it may be that people simply eat more vegetables when the veggies are sautéed in a little bit of olive oil or roasted with a few splashes of toasted sesame oil. The added fat also improves absorption of health-enhancing phytochemicals in plant foods. But beyond that, certain oils have their own health-promoting qualities. Extra-virgin olive oil, for example, contains unique phytochemicals that are related to a decreased risk of heart disease, hypertension, and breast cancer. That peppery "bite" you experience when tasting high-quality olive oil comes from oleocanthal, a compound that may have powerful anti-inflammatory and anticancer effects.

Keep in mind that quality of extra-virgin olive oil varies greatly. Look for extra-virgin olive oil that is packaged in a dark glass bottle and that has a harvest or "best by" date on it. An estate name on the label is a good sign that you are purchasing quality olive oil, too. You don't need to pay a fortune for good olive oil; check the Truth in Olive Oil website (www.truthinoliveoil.com) for a list of recommended olive oil brands that are available in supermarkets.

Walnut oil also has demonstrated health benefits and is associated with reduced blood levels of harmful triglycerides. Soybean and walnut oils are unique because they provide high amounts of both omega-6 and omega-3 fatty acids. The omega-6 fats reduce cholesterol levels while omega-3 fats have anti-inflammatory properties.

None of this is to say that oil is a dietary essential. Some people prefer to cook without it and that's fine. It's just good to know that if you want to enjoy the recipes in this book that use a little bit of oil, it's okay to do so.

If you cook with oil, there are a couple of things to keep in mind. Cold-pressed or expeller-pressed oils are extracted from nuts and seeds through mechanical crushing and pressing. These oils are typically higher in antioxidants and other phytochemicals than refined oils. They also have a richer flavor. However, they are more susceptible to rancidity so they should always be kept in the refrigerator. If you use very little oil and the bottle lasts for a long time, you can even freeze them. Try freezing oil in ice cube trays so you can defrost just a little bit at a time.

It's also important to pay attention to smoke point, which is the temperature at which an oil begins to break down and decompose. Generally, refined oils have a higher smoke point so they are best for cooking at high temperatures. But even among refined oils, smoke point varies.

For omega-3 fats such as hempseed and flaxseed oils, just 1 teaspoon flaxseed oil or 1 1/2 teaspoons hempseed oil will provide the necessary daily dose of this essential nutrient. These oils are fragile, though. Keep them in the refrigerator and never heat them.

Common Vegetable Oils and Ideal Cooking Temperatures	
Temperature	Oil
High-temperature cooking (400°F to 450°F)	Refined soy oil; peanut oil; sunflower oil; corn oil; safflower oil; avocado oil; light olive oil
Moderate-temperature cooking (400°F and lower)	Refined coconut oil; canola oil (refined or expeller-pressed); expeller-pressed avocado oil; grapeseed oil
Low-temperature cooking (350°F and lower)	Cold-pressed sesame oil; virgin coconut oil; good quality extra-virgin olive oil
Flavoring, drizzling, and finishing or cooking at very low heat (320°F and lower)	Expeller-pressed nut oils like walnut, almond, and macadamia; toasted sesame oil

Common Whole-Foods Cooking Times

Food	Amount	Time (in minutes)	Cooking Temperature (in °F)	Shake	Extra Information
Homemade Fries (thin sticks)	10–35 ounces	22–50	392	Shake	Optional: Toss fries in 1 teaspoon extra-virgin olive oil or canola oil
Homemade Potato Wedges	10–28 ounces	20–28	392	Shake	Optional: Toss wedges in 1 teaspoon extra-virgin olive oil or canola oil
Homemade Potato Cubes	10–26 ounces	20–28	356	Shake	Optional: Toss cubes in 1 teaspoon extra-virgin olive oil or canola oil
Whole Baked Potatoes	4 medium	20	390	Turn	Set for 15 minutes, turn potatoes, cook 5 more minutes (add more time for more potatoes)
Artichoke Hearts	12 ounces frozen	10	350	Shake	Coat with lemon juice, oil, salt and pepper, and seasonings of choice
Brussels Sprouts	Any amount	12	400	Shake	Cook plain or add a mist or two of vegetable spray and/or toss in balsamic vinegar
Roasted Garlic	1 bulb	15	320	No shaking needed	Turn the bulb upside down, take off most of the outer husk, cut off the bottom of the bulb, drizzle with olive oil, and wrap in foil
Green Beans	About 2 cups	10	375	Shake	Coat with olive oil, salt, and pepper
Peppers (poblano, pasilla, shishito etc.)		5–10	390	Shake	Spray the peppers with oil, add salt, pepper, garlic, or other spices
Zucchini	1 small or medium, sliced into rounds	10	375	Shake	Toss with just a few drops of olive oil; coat with panko bread crumbs

More Ways to Use the Air Fryer

I started the Facebook group, Vegan Air Frying Enthusiasts, as soon as I bought my first air fryer. The group members and I have fun sharing cooking techniques and "hacks" with one another. Here are some of our favorites:

- Melt nondairy butter in a small ramekin for baking or making a sauce: 30 seconds at 390°F.

- Toast frozen bagels: 3 minutes at 390°F.

- Toast bread: 2 minutes at 360°F.

- Warm soft corn or flour tortillas by layering them, with parchment paper between each tortilla, and wrap in foil: 10 minutes at 330°F.

- Cook almost any Gardein brand frozen food: 8 to 10 minutes at 390°F.

- Cook frozen vegan egg rolls and pot stickers (readily available at Asian markets): 10 minutes at 390°F.

- Cook frozen vegan burgers: 10 to 15 minutes at 390°F.

- Make a grilled cheese sandwich with 2 pieces of bread and 1 to 2 slices nondairy cheese. Spread nondairy butter on one side of each piece of bread and place the sandwich in the air fryer, buttered sides facing out: 3 minutes on 390°F.

- Reheat leftovers in the air fryer instead of a microwave. Simply add the food to an air fryer–safe bowl or pan: 5 to 10 minutes at 360°F or 390°F.

- Perk up restaurant carryout or delivery. Simply place fried or baked food in the air fryer to warm it and make it crunchy again: 5 minutes at 360°F.

If you can bake it, you can probably air-fry it. While there is no hard and fast conversion, I have found that air-frying at close to the same temperature recommended for conventional baking while reducing the cooking time by half works pretty well. Give it a try!

Online Resources

- **JL's website:** jlgoesvegan.com

- **Vegan Air Frying Enthusiasts Facebook group:** https://www.facebook.com/groups/TheVeganAirFryer/

- **FatFree Vegan Air Fryers Facebook group:** https://www.facebook.com/groups/FatFreeVeganAF/

Air Fryer Brands

My first air fryer was the GoWISE 4th generation 3.7-quart. This size was ideal for our two-person household. I added the Philips Avance XL to my air-frying arsenal because I wanted to work with a large basket that could hold a variety of accessories for creating recipes. I then added two other models: the Farberware (exclusive to Walmart), which was the exact same size as the GoWISE, and a much smaller Simply Ming. My recipes work beautifully in all four models, but you'll clearly have more flexibility with a larger device, particularly if you want to layer food in the air fryer or use accessories such as a baking pan or casserole dish.

I enlisted a good number of recipe testers for this cookbook and they used a variety of models including Cook's Essential, Elite Platinum, Farberware, GoWISE (four different models), and three different models of Philips.

I moderate a Facebook group dedicated to vegan air frying. At the time I was writing this cookbook, we had nearly 5,000 members. I asked the group to share which air fryer brands they use:

- Avalon Bay
- Bella
- Black & Decker
- Cooks Companion
- Cook's Essentials
- Farberware
- Force
- Gourmia
- GoWISE
- Kalorik
- Lidore
- NuWave Brio
- Philips
- Power Air Fryer XL
- Rosewill
- Simply Ming
- T-fal ActiFry

Acknowledgements

First and foremost, thank you to Jon Robertson and the Vegan Heritage Press team. I am a longtime fan of the quality vegan cookbooks produced by Vegan Heritage Press, and it's my utmost honor to now be among the authors I've admired for so long. Jon's leadership and appreciation for an author's unique voice and vision is special. I am grateful.

Michelle Donner, the brilliant photographer for this book, is a dream come true. With humor, passion, and a creative eye, she made each dish with love and enthusiasm. She is a skilled professional and a woman I'm honored to call a very dear friend.

Ginny Messina, my coauthor of *Vegan for Her,* is the reason I was able to become a "professional vegan." (Because what's better than spending every single waking hour focused on furthering a vegan message and changing the world for animals?) Ginny is the reason I'm a happy, healthy vegan with zero hang-ups about body size. When I asked her to write the piece on oil she said yes, bought an air fryer, and tested recipes. What a friend. What a voice of reason. What a force of nature.

I am so grateful for my recipe testers. You guys! You were right there, diligent and dedicated, and your input was invaluable. Thank you to Alison, Amy, Betsey, Bettina, Bonnie, Ginny, Jana, Joy, Kellin, Kristi, Kristy, Lauren, Leslie, Lora, Melissa, Michelle, Mike, Rachael, Rhonda, Sara, Shirley, Sue, and Tamara.

To the Vegan Air Frying Enthusiasts Facebook group members: Michelle and I are so honored to moderate a group filled with like-minded culinary wizards creating and sharing ideas for air fryer creations. Such a compassionate community.

Thanks to GoWISE and Philips for providing appliances to help me test recipes for this book. And thanks to GoWISE and the Idaho Potato Commission for partnering with me to take air frying cooking classes across the United States!

To my sisters Dana and Dee Ann for jumping on the air-frying bandwagon and texting me photos of their vegan creations, thank you! And my mom and dad, Janice and Larry; niece Paige; and Aunt Candy eagerly nibbled on my air-fried bites, too. Thank you!

At the time I write this book, the animal companions in my life are Ernie and Oliver. They are impossibly bossy cats and they are impossible not to love. I am, forever, a crazy cat lady.

My heart bursts for my husband, Dave. He has been my biggest cheerleader since we met in 1996. Not only does he support every single nutty idea I have, he's usually right next to me, helping me make it happen.

And finally, thanks to the one and only reason I write vegan cookbooks: the animals.

About the Author

JL Fields is an author, culinary instructor, columnist, speaker, activist, and radio personality. She is the founder and director of the Colorado Springs Vegan Cooking Academy, the author of *Vegan Pressure Cooking: Delicious Beans, Grains and One-Pot Meals in Minutes,* and co-author of *Vegan for Her: The Woman's Guide to Being Healthy and Fit on a Plant-Based Diet.* She is also a brands consultant for a variety of national companies and food associations. The publisher of JL Goes Vegan.com, JL has received culinary training at the Natural Gourmet Institute and the Christina Pirello School of Natural Cooking and Integrative Health Studies. She is a Main Street Vegan Academy-certified Vegan Lifestyle Coach and Educator and a certified Food for Life instructor with Physicians Committee for Responsible Medicine (PCRM). She writes and broadcasts from Colorado Springs, Colorado.

Website: www.jlgoesvegan.com
facebook.com/jlgoesvegan
twitter.com/jlgoesvegan
instagram.com/jlgoesvegan
pinterest.com/jlgoesvegan/

Vegan Air Frying Enthusiasts Facebook group: https://www.facebook.com/groups/TheVeganAirFryer/

Index

The Vegan Air Fryer

Metric Conversions and Equivalents

The recipes in this book have not been tested with metric measurements, so some variations may occur.

LIQUID	
US	**METRIC**
1 tsp	5 ml
1 tbs	15 ml
2 tbs	30 ml
1/4 cup	60 ml
1/3 cup	75 ml
1/2 cup	120 ml
2/3 cup	150 ml
3/4 cup	180 ml
1 cup	240 ml
1 1/4 cups	300 ml
1 1/3 cups	325 ml
1 1/2 cups	350 ml
1 2/3 cups	375 ml
1 3/4 cups	400 ml
2 cups (1 pint)	475 ml
3 cups	720 ml
4 cups (1 quart)	945 ml

GENERAL METRIC CONVERSION FORMULAS	
Ounces to grams	ounces x 28.35 = grams
Grams to ounces	grams x 0.035 = ounces
Pounds to grams	pounds x 435.5 = grams
Pounds to kilograms	pounds x 0.45 = kilograms
Cups to liters	cups x 0.24 = liters
Fahrenheit to Celsius	($°F - 32$) x 5 ÷ 9 = $°C$
Celsius to Fahrenheit	($°C$ x 9) ÷ 5 + 32 = $°F$

WEIGHT	
US	**METRIC**
1/2 oz	14 g
1 oz	28 g
1 1/2 oz	43 g
2 oz	57 g
2 1/2 oz	71 g
4 oz	113 g
5 oz	142 g
6 oz	170 g
7 oz	200 g
8 oz (1/2 lb)	227 g
9 oz	255 g
10 oz	284 g
11 oz	312 g
12 oz	340 g
13 oz	368 g
14 oz	400 g
15 oz	425 g
16 oz (1 lb)	454 g

OVEN TEMPERATURE		
°F	**Gas Mark**	**°C**
250	1/2	120
275	1	140
300	2	150
325	3	165
350	4	180
375	5	190
400	6	200
425	7	220
450	8	230
475	9	240
500	10	260
550	Broil	290

LENGTH	
US	**METRIC**
1/2 inch	1.25 cm
1 inch	2.5 cm
6 inches	15 cm
8 inches	20 cm
10 inches	25 cm
12 inches	30 cm